THE MAN WHO LOVED DRAGONS

Other books by Trevor Hay

Tartar City Woman: Scenes from the Life of Wang Hsin-Ping, Former Citizen of China, Melbourne University Press, 1990, biography, history.

East Wind, West Wind, (with Fang Xiangshu) Penguin, 1992, biography.

Black Ice : A Story of Modern China, Trevor Hay, (with Fang Xiangshu), Indra Publishing, 1997, novel, historical fiction.

China's Proletarian Myth: The Revolutionary Narrative and Model Theatre of the Cultural Revolution, Lambert Academic Publishing, 2008, Chinese theatre and politics.

A Dream of Red Dragonflies. A Strange Tale of China, the World — and a Third Place, Tantanoola, Australian Scholarly Publishing, 2016, novel.

Letters from a Floating Life, Tantanoola, Australian Scholarly Publishing, 2017, novel.

The Secret of the Lunar Rainbow, Tantanoola, Australian Scholarly Publishing, 2018, novel.

Redgrave's Ghost, Tantanoola, Australian Scholarly Publishing, 2019, novel.

The Tengu: Tales from the Temple of Ordinary Terrors, Tantanoola, Australian Scholarly Publishing, novel, 2020.

The Library of Lost Horizons. An Antiquarian Voyage, Arden, Australian Scholarly Publishing, 2023.

THE MAN WHO LOVED DRAGONS

My China Curios and the Gates of Dreams

TREVOR HAY

MELBOURNE & GALWAY
www.scholarly.info

First published in 2024 by ARDEN
a literary imprint of Australian Scholarly Publishing Pty Ltd

7 Lt Lothian St Nth, North Melbourne, Victoria 3051
tel 03 9329 6963
contact@scholarly.info / www.scholarly.info

ISBN: 978-1-923267-03-9

Cover design and typesetting:
Luke Harris, WorkingType Studio

Cover illustration shows jewellery from the Imperial Palace Museum Shop, Beijing, provided by Ms. Peng Shanshan, (彭闪闪), Executive President of the Intangible Cultural Heritage Association (非物质文化遗产协会).

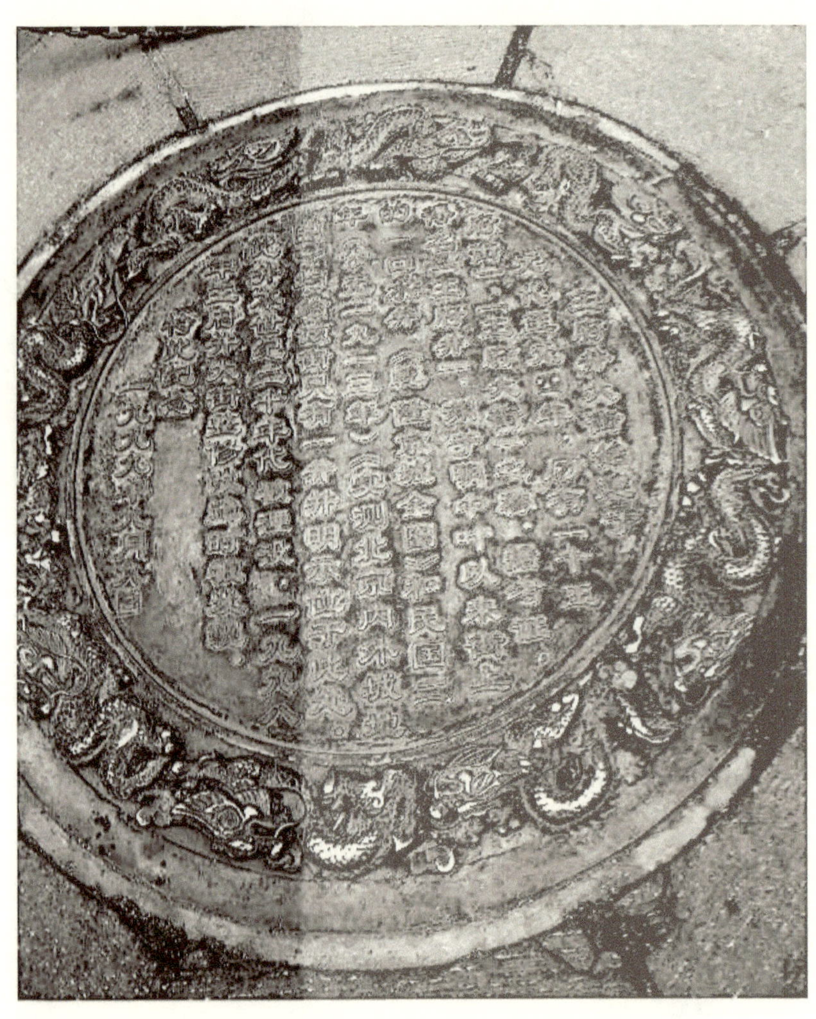

My 2017 photo of a much-overlooked curio of 'Old Peking' is shown on facing page. This is the well-cover commemorating the site of the old well in Wangfujing Dajie, 王府井大街, The Street of the Well of the Prince's Mansion, once known by foreigners as 'Morrison Street', after its famous resident G.E. Morrison, (1862-1920), the Australian journalist, *Times* correspondent, epic walker, collector of books on China, adventurer, participant in the defence of the Legation during the Boxer Uprising and adviser to the President of the Republic of China during the First World War. He once lived at number 98 on the same, that is west, side of the road. The characters record the date of the installation of the cover, a date featuring an auspicious number for dragons, 9/9/99. Note the dragons on the rim, nine if I'm not mistaken. The street is now an 'unmissable shopping destination' for both Chinese and foreign tourists. Cosmetics and ladies' shoes are prominent but men are not forgotten and might get even more than they bargained for if they linger in response to a young lady's opening gambit, 'Hello. Where are you from?'. Males of the Australian kind might try saying, 'the same place as George Morrison'. That might give just enough time to extract themselves from the wiles of the modern variety of Old Peking's 'fox-nymphs'. Unless, of course, curiosity gets the better of them.

For Ye Hong, 叶洪, 'Little Leaf',
who shares a family name with
the man who loved dragons …
but who is herself afraid of nothing.

Acknowledgements

Writing a book is always hard work, but this one showed its true nature when it thought I wasn't looking, like the *hulijing* in the stories of 'Old Peking'.

Coaxing it out of its lair was greatly assisted with the help of some expert friends, including

- the advice, resources, IT expertise and mentoring of master librarian and bibliophile David Cunnington, with whom I have shared many curious moments in China;

- the many privileged years of collaboration, travel and inspiring conversation with Professor Joseph Lo Bianco AM, during our far-flung research into the teaching of Chinese language and culture;

- the help of Ms. Peng Shanshan (彭闪闪) of the Intangible Cultural Heritage and Arts Association in deciphering the mysterious bamboo poem;

* the documentary material provided by my colleague Dr Catherine Wang (王永阳) for the chapter on the monastery in Guizhou

* and the usual beguiling cover design, typesetting and photographic enhancement of Luke Harris of WorkingType Studio.

A Note on Spelling

Ralph Waldo Emerson warned us about 'foolish consistency', and T.E. Lawrence was pretty scornful of it when it came to the transliteration of Arabic words. That's my defence for the irregularities that occur within. Chinese orthography of the modern PRC kind is certainly one of Emerson's 'hobgoblins' when it comes to place names, and the way the components are organised. I try to keep place names like *Yuan Ming Yuan* and *Xuan Wu Men* arranged in separate capitalised units of meaning for the same reason I do not spell The South China Sea as Thesouthchinasea, but there are times when it is all too difficult. That's why the Chinese use characters.

One thing that's relatively easy to explain in response to a FAQ. I sometimes use Beijing, and sometimes Peking. It all depends on the atmosphere.

Contents

Forethoughts

We do not know what the dragon *means*, just as we do not know the meaning of the universe, but there is something in the image of the dragon that is congenial to man's imagination, and thus the dragon arises in many latitudes and ages. It is, one might say, a *necessary monster*, not some ephemeral and casual creature like the chimaera or the catoblepas.
Jose Luis Borges and Margarita Guerrero, Foreword,
The Book of Imaginary Beings, 1954.

True, the sacred dragon stands on the little column at the end of our village, and ever since the beginning of human memory it has breathed out its fiery breath in the direction of Peking in token of homage – but Peking itself is far stranger to the people in our village than the next world.
Franz Kafka, *The Great Wall of China*.

I have written of things that are beyond our grasp yet visible
to all, dear to our hearts and far from our understanding
as the constellations; a comfort for the frail light they shed.
Without being astronomers, in our separate darkness, we
rejoice in them, and from our caves, our twilights of belief
and ignorant names and lonely journeys, feel that we are a
fellowship that looks to the same stars.
Freya Stark, *Perseus in the Wind.*

I have a sort of horror of Australia, although I have never
been there except for a few hours in Melbourne on my way
from Bombay to Los Angeles by boat in 1943.
Bob Winter, Letters, 8 November, 1970.

1.   The Sea-chest

When I was a little girl and was taken to see my grandmother, she set out for my amusement, to be looked at but not touched by little fingers, various curios brought home by my grandfather from China in the old days when he was a sailor in the Honourable East India Company's service; beautifully carved ivory chessmen, a model of a Chinese lady's foot about three inches long, dainty mother-of-pearl counters made in the likeness of all manner of strange beasts, lacquer boxes and ivory balls; models of palankeens [palanquins] in ivory and fans that seemed to me, brought up in the somewhat rough-and-ready surroundings of a new country, [Australia, 'new' in terms of white settlement] dreams of loveliness. The impression was made, I felt the fascination of China, the fascination of a thing far beyond me.

So wrote Mary Gaunt, Australian novelist, intrepid traveller in the West Indies, West Africa and China at the turn of the twentieth century, rather less-than-enthusiastically-acknowledged relative by marriage to famed Australian journalist, diplomat and adventurer G.E. ('Chinese') Morrison, and a lady herself destined to travel in 'palankeens' for which she was clearly not designed and for which her coolies could hardly have been prepared. Her recollection strikes a chord with me as I gaze around my study. Many of the authors on the shelves have been enticed into foreign travel by this quality of 'fascination' – and the most writerly of them, including Mary at times, manage to capture something of the thrill of being simultaneously attracted and repelled by strangeness. The fascination of China often starts out like this, with the lure of a curio – 'a thing beyond'.

And what could be more fascinating or more Chinese than dragons? There's many a Chinese proverb about them but my favourite concerns a certain Ye Gong of old who couldn't get enough of them, but then when a real one intruded into his sanctuary it frightened him witless. In one of my explanations of popular Chinese aphorisms the last line reads 'What Lord Ye Gong loved were fake dragons painted on the walls and carved on the pillars, not real dragons'. This seems a trite and censorious summary of a much deeper irony. Ai Weiwei, the contemporary Chinese artist and activist, tells the story much better in his 'graphic memoir', *Zodiac* (2024). In this version, an artist professes a desire to meet a dragon, who then obliges by visiting him in his studio. On seeing the dragon, the painter flees in fear, and the narrator, Ai Weiwei, who by now has himself assumed some characteristics of the dragon, reminds us that 'it is important to think about what you really desire. It could kill you.'

What is a 'real' dragon? I certainly haven't made a career out of 'fake dragons' when it comes to China. I've sweated ink for decades pursuing something of her elusive reality, yet, as a foreigner, it's only when I've come close to Chinese *people*, rather than the place called China that I have even been aware of the 'real' thing. There have been many times when that has been difficult, even frightening. Here be not only dragons, but the possibility – likelihood – of mistakes, of painful encounters and misunderstandings, of humiliating failures, and intermittent retreats to my sanctuary. Sometimes that sanctuary was within China, in the home of a friend in the suburbs of Beijing, or in the *Baoli* Hot Springs 'health resort' on the outskirts of the much less frequently-visited south-western city of Guiyang; sometimes it was in a dingy, damp room on the campus of a river town university. And sometimes, when it was all too much, after a long spell in China, it was a studio apartment on the Eltham-Yarra Glen Road, in a place appropriately named 'The Gateway'. That proved ideal as a form of de-compression, because, as if to anticipate my needs, I found on return one year that the hotel had been taken over and staffed by Chinese. After he got to know me, the boss, Tiger Wang, would even welcome me back with a couple of glasses of XO brandy and a feed of dumplings. I don't get that in Australian hotels. Or in Chinese. You have to be an in-between person to get the best of both worlds.

My first non-book dragons were encountered not in China but in the South Australian Museum, North Terrace, Adelaide – two whale skeletons that were displayed like tutelary gods at the entrance. My ten-year old imagination of their possibilities was accompanied by a sense of magic not to be diminished by any scientific explanation of what they *really* were. They became a permanent exhibit in the *wunderkammer* taking shape in my mind. Their spell did not diminish with the frequency of my visits as I added the flesh of knowledge to their bones but I'm sure they wouldn't have had anything like that first impact if they had been fully restored or digitally-animated virtual whales.

There's a late seventeenth century painting, *Cabinet des Merveilles*, 'Cabinet of Curiosities', by Andrea Domenico Remps, in which a wardrobe opens to reveal paintings of ships hung on the inside of the doors, and you then gaze through another partially opened – and cracked – glass door into shelves of ostensibly random curiosities of skulls, feathers, coral, globes, watches and looking-glasses. Tricking the eye into 'seeing things' has long been a multi-media art form, both elite and vulgar, from ancient Greek temples to seaside carnival side-shows of the nineteenth century – the art and science of provoking the imagination of the viewer. I like the idea, inherent in these displays, which encompass the spectacle of early museum and freak show, that polite discourse did not permit too much precision – or too much speculation-killing certainty – in contemplating the closet, or chamber, of marvels. Participation in the game required the preservation of wonder. By way of example, a seventeenth century English father and son team had a collection called Tradescant's Ark, containing 'oriental footwear, a mermaid's hand, a dragon's egg, two feathers of a phoenix's tail, a piece of the True Cross and a vial of blood that rained on the Isle of Wight'.

But what could be more curious, in all its senses, more stimulating of the imagination, more attested to in a haphazard collection of science, superstition and souvenir, more subject to tricks of perspective, more sustained in ambivalence, than the meeting/ collision of East and West, so often symbolised by a dragon, not only in the sleeping dragon metaphor attributed to Napoleon, but on the covers of books from the eighteenth to twenty-first centuries? More recently book covers feature the trope of a 'rising dragon' on volumes laden with advice for would-be foreign entrepreneurs and political strategists. The multi-clawed and coiled dragon, its international counterparts in mythology and folklore notwithstanding, has been an abiding symbol of Chinese cultural identity since the earliest east-west contacts, rather than a symbol of military threat or economic opportunity, as in its most common contemporary guise.

I confess to feeling superior at times to my ten-year old self and to the likes of Lord Ye Gong and all those who have chosen to stick with their dragons of magic and folklore and their monster-myth video games, but, with advanced age and its various ways of bringing you down a peg or two, I've come to see things differently. You have to start somewhere, to swim within the flags of 'fascination' before you strike out into the deep of difference. And so what if you don't make it that far, or don't want to, as long as you don't think that's all there is? For most of us, 'fairy tales' are our first exposure to magic and enchantment, and no matter how much we manage to interpret its more sophisticated sibling – myth – as a coherent genre with its roots in the collective human psyche, it is the weirdness and scariness of the crude old folktale that first lures us and then, if we are ready, entices us further afield. There are two observations about the distinction between myth and fairy tale that inform the way I'm thinking about curios in this book. The first is by Walter Benjamin, the German Marxist philosopher and cultural critic: 'The fairy tale tells us of the earliest arrangements that mankind made to shake off the nightmare which the myth had placed upon its chest'. And the second is by Marie-Louise von Franz, in her Jungian interpretation of fairy tales, in which, in contrast to many folklorists who regard fairy tales as a 'degenerate' form of myth, she regards them as *basic* to myth, the 'sea' from which 'waves' of mythology arise. The dragon, of course, is at home anywhere, and in China often takes the form of 'Long Wang', the Dragon King of seas and rivers, bringer of rain, protector of seafarers. As for the ambivalence – wisdom – of both loving and fearing dragons, G. K. Chesterton came close to the source when he said, somewhere, probably in the *London Illustrated News*, 'Fairy tales do not tell children the dragons exist. Children already know that dragons exist. Fairy tales tell children the dragons can be killed.'

That word 'fascination' pops up immediately whenever people look back on whatever got them started in anything from bird-watching to quantum physics, and it inevitably comes up when people ask me how – why – I got interested in China, as if there were a single cause, like Mary's ivory chessmen. It may have been that obliging dragon in my old Rupert Bear annuals, but that's not what people want to hear, so I usually make something up. I did have a great-uncle, Able Seaman Herbert Thomas Hill (1874-1958), who served on Her Majesty's Colonial Ship *Protector*, based in Port Adelaide until 1900, after which, as part of the Colonial Naval Service, she sailed for China and the river forts of the Boxer Uprising.

There's a shot of the crew on the facing page, and I think that's Uncle Herbie second from far right, second row. He had a long

face and lantern jaw, like Randolph Scott. By the time *Protector* got there the Boxers had left, but my Uncle Herbie, suitor to my Grandma Violet, remains the first person I ever knew who had been to China, and there's a relic of his service among my curiosities, a medal inscribed 'China 1900'.

HMCS *Protector* came to an ignominious end in 1943 when she collided with a tug in the waters of the southern Great Barrier Reef and was subsequently sunk off Heron Island for use as a breakwater. One of her four-ton, six-inch guns was – still is – located on The Esplanade at Semaphore Beach, Adelaide, and afforded great adventure of the post-Saturday-afternoon-matinee-movie kind to the pirate-buccaneer-Captain Blood kids of my circle. To my surprise the fabled galleon of my youth and my first 'real' introduction to China turned up once more when I was watching

David Attenborough doing a documentary on the destruction of birdlife caused by a tropical storm on the island. There she was, an unlikely participant in the story of Australia and China, serving as unremarked background to Sir David's footage on the devastation wreaked by Nature upon the nests of black noddy terns.

There's another curio representing the history of maritime dealings between China and the West in my study, a painting (shown above), oil on canvas, of a nineteenth-century British barque.

You can see the white cliffs of Dover in the background, there's another barque turning leeward into the harbour and there's a hybrid steamer in the distance on the other side of the painting, puffing smoke but carrying two masts for sail, a portent of the demise of the great days of the clippers that would come with completion of the Suez Canal in 1869. J. Murday, a noted maritime artist of the nineteenth century, has signed the painting but the date is very hard to read, perhaps 1839. According to the website *MutualArt*, Murday died in the 1860s and he seems to have painted several scenes of a similar nature during the 1830s and 1840s. There's no name on this ship, no plaque on the painting, although there is a very similar work by Murday, titled *"Castor" off the cliffs of Dover on her voyage to the South Sea Fishery, 1833*. Since no other name is visible, I can take my pick from a list of British vessels in Basil Lubbock's *The China Clippers*, (1914) and call her 'Silver Eagle'. She reminds me of a great white migratory bird, always skimming the ocean, flying between continents, coming to rest on isolated outcrops of landfall. In my mind she 'rides the winds and cleaves the seas', as the Chinese say, a symbol of China-West encounters – illusions and fantasies, dreams and shadows, delights and fears.

The painting's previous owner was a descendant of one of the vessel's skippers, and although I have no detail from him, I suppose the ship was involved in the China trade, probably bringing tea from China to Britain, and taking opium to China from India. She may have carried a more mundane drug of addiction – grog of various sorts. She may have been a whaler, like 'Castor', or she may once have been a slaver, ultimately condemned by anti-slavery legislation in Britain and the United States, but then adroitly diversifying to the opium trade.

Also in my study is a sea-chest that belonged to the captain of that same clipper. Among the things in the chest are two pipes; one long wooden carved pipe, about a metre long, which has an open bowl and still contains almost fossilised ash – you can actually smell it, suggesting it was used for tobacco rather than opium, although it may have contained both. The other one, some kind of horn, is beautifully carved with bats, dragons and little boys, a genuine opium pipe, with a bowl that can be unscrewed, into which you insert a pill of opium and apply the heat of a small lamp in order to inhale the vapour – it's more like 'vaping' than smoking. I'm still looking to see if I can acquire a full opium set, with the lamp and other paraphernalia. I'm not a user, but the pipe does lead me into a kind of hallucinatory state. I inhale a dream as I gaze at it, and I hear a distant echo of my all-female orchestra of musical figurines glazed in Tang 'egg-and-spinach' style, sitting on top of the chest. I try to imagine the chest in ever-receding images, inside the painting, inside the clipper, inside the cabin, inside its own time. My clipper isn't the famed 'Cutty Sark' kind, with three billowing clouds of square-rigged sails, but what I take to be a barque, a three-masted, ocean-going, wooden-hulled sailing ship with two jibs or headsails attached to a long spear-like bowsprit, her foremast and mainsail square-rigged, that is with sails square to the keel, and a mizzen mast with spanker, gaff-rigged, the sails and yards in the same plane as the keel, aligned fore and aft. There are eight crew members visible on deck, but there are seven gunports on the port side, suggesting that certain past activities of the vessel might have required rather more manpower.

Memories are roused from my own fifty years of travel in China, and something of the painfully liberating ordeal of learning Chinese, a process akin to the shamanic rituals of breaking down an old body in order to acquire a new soul. Alastair Morrison, son of George, reluctant relative of Mary Gaunt, has this to say concerning the process:

> …to acquire a first-class knowledge of both the written and spoken language is a lifetime's study. To reach the standard of an educated Chinese is something that is rarely achieved by a Westerner, and the few who try generally become very queer in the attempt.

Given my late start in learning Chinese, my only experience of a language other than English being Latin, French and army drill instructors, I suppose I must have been queer to begin with. Becoming *very* queer started in the 1970s with serious study and what might be considered 'field trips', often culminating in an illustrated talk, with a carousel of Kodachrome slides, little windows to China in which I made the most of a limited understanding of the things I had photographed with scant fear of being contradicted – although I do remember one indignant viewer protesting that I seemed to have nothing but good things to say about China. While I was scornful of his attitude at the time, he may well have had a point. You can be right for the wrong reasons, and vice-versa. In this present slide-show I have chosen not what is good or bad, but things that may require viewers to adjust their perspective, a process rather like those 3-D puzzles you used to see, curios in themselves, where you had to stare into a pattern and get your eyes out of focus before you could see the picture inside the pattern. The key to seeing *through* the pattern *into* the picture, getting your eyes out of 'focus' in order to do so, is a special viewing device – the curio. It can be a two-way device, enabling a foreigner to discern the patterns of cultural constellations in a Chinese cosmos, or enabling a Chinese person to read the sky as a foreigner does.

As it happens, for me, the things most worthy of the title 'curio' are not just puzzles, or objects, but events, imaginings and strange tales inscribed in books of another age, many of which might well be subject to heavy editing or eliminated altogether from libraries by the requirements of modern ideological hygiene. In any case, whether the viewing device is an arcane artefact, a clouded memory, a whole book of travel memoirs, a recurring dream, a painting, a piece of music, a postcard, a map or a photograph, it may well remain merely a thing of inexplicable fascination, but an eye that has learned to see differently may gradually transform it from amorphous oddity into a source of understanding.

I'm thinking now of the way nameless emotions of the past rise, coil and vanish like smoke-signals from embers of buried memory. I once invited a charming female colleague, an Italian music teacher, to dinner at my place. We had been discussing *Turandot* and Orientalism and I thought to impress her with a sort of musical collage that illustrated our discussion. I began with Ketèlby's *In a Chinese Temple Garden*. She asked me, almost immediately, if I could *please* play something else. She explained – it was a kind of premonition; as soon as she heard one of Ketèlby's bells or gongs start up she had a sinking feeling something awful would follow. She had a funny look on her face as she said this. I can see it now, and, after all these years, I am finally able to read it not as anxiety but as an invitation to appreciate her droll remark. At the time however, it was wasted on a mind preoccupied with fanciful romance beyond any of Ketèlbey's Persian markets or bells across the meadows. I pressed on with *The Butterfly Lovers* violin concerto, considering her behaviour disappointingly superstitious in an educated woman. I didn't realise there are plenty of people who have similar reactions to Albert Ketèlby and it has nothing to do with superstition. The point is though, as I look back I see that I've often been contemptuous of superstition in those of Western cultural background while maintaining a non-judgemental, ethnographic objectivity in my attitude to Chinese friends who wear talismans to protect themselves from evil spirits, or rotate Buddhist rosary beads between their knuckles and mumble mantras while sitting on planes. I see too that I have been critical of people who believe in gods and saints and devils, while keeping an open mind about the 'paranormal'. In loving dragons of any kind, and collecting them, there's always a danger you will lose balance. Sometimes, as in this memory of my Italian musician, it's a slight matter, but there are many examples of very serious consequences, individual and national, in the history of intercultural encounters between China and the world.

Like William Lindesay, author of *The Great Wall in 50 Objects* (Penguin, 2015), I have thought carefully about the common nature of the things I've included for contemplation: 'Though a scattered and disparate lot, the items investigated shared a common quality: all were storytelling objects.' Having worked and travelled in China on and off for some years as the guest of a Chinese/international Intangible Cultural Heritage Association (非物质文化遗产协会),

I have been drawn to the storytelling potential of things intangible, confirmed in so doing by Lindesay's inclusion of the wolf-dung smoke said to have been used on the Han Dynasty Great Wall beacons of the Gobi to alert the sentries to the approach of the terrifying 'Hun' (*Xiongnu*) cavalry. I've heard that the heady odour preceding the arrival of the Huns was warning enough. Anyway, smoke and mirrors, memories and illusions, all legitimate contents for my own Cabinet de Merveilles. As I get older I'm losing the ability – or the will – to distinguish between the fragments of truth preserved in memory and the fiction that my writer-in-residence has created of these fragments. My memory is a fragile old journal with some pages missing, some browning and foxing and a good few indecipherable notes scribbled in the margins by a previous owner.

Conceptually, there is no clearer beginning and end to the stories than in that ring of bronze dragons guarding the Prince's Well in Beijing, but they are conveyed by a narrative vehicle even more marvellous than Rupert's dragon, enabling the reader to descend through and across time, from recent history of individual interaction between Chinese and foreigners to the 'collision of civilisations' from the eighteenth to the twentieth centuries and back again into antiquity with an art form bearing a script of the third millennium BCE. It may appear there is no more over-arching order here than in the items selected by Mary's grandmother, but in defence of my cabinet of curiosities I quote Wilfrid J. Blunt, botanist, artist, author, teacher and traveller in the Middle East and Central Asia in the mid-twentieth century:

The book may be considered as a series of tableaux, selected to suit a personal taste yet in the hope that they may chance to suit the taste of others also. I have, as it were, gone to a heavily-laden apple tree and picked a handful of easily-accessible ripe fruit which took my fancy.

Or it may be a 'gallimaufry', a word I had never encountered until it bobbed up in the vocabulary of two authors whose works are linked by a tragic and horrifying tale to come. You could Google it, but that would deprive it of curiosity value. In any case, I hope this book will prove to be the beginning of curiosity, perhaps even fascination, for some.

2. Who but the Chinese?

I'm adrift, imagining …the sea-chest does that for me; when I gaze at it early in the morning I'm transported, it saves me waiting until mid-afternoon to be fully delusional. Things are moving around on that chest. I know very well there was an antique silver hairpin next to the carved wooden monkey clutching an armful of corn, spilling cobs as he tries to gather more, a symbol of self-defeating greed, or perhaps of an endearing lust for life, as much a symbol of humanity as of monkey business. He seems to be alive. The Japanese have a name for some curios – *tsukumogami* – meaning ostensibly inanimate objects that acquire the force of life over time. If an object gets to be one hundred years old it can come to life and amuse itself playing tricks on its owner. Since I have lots of things at least a hundred years old, I'm particularly vulnerable. I may even be an apprentice *tsukumogami* myself.

If I were a Ming dynasty teller of ghost stories I would say there was a strand of hair wrapped around the little silver bells that hung from the hairpin, and that strand has now reassembled itself into the spirit of its former owner. The spirit-woman has gone in search of the silk-gowned ladies painted on the fan that sits in the lower drawer of the sea-chest. They're perched together on a perforated, fern-laced rock in their sequestered boudoir, surrounded by peonies and azaleas, behind them is a marble balustrade and a lotus-coated pond, beyond that are palms and an arched stone bridge flanked by a wall enclosing another pavilion. One of the ladies holds a fan and one is wearing – my missing hairpin.

On the sea-chest sits a round yellow object on a sandalwood base. It sits a little insecurely, hiding the base because, being a thing of nature, it is asymmetrical. It's a gourd, or part of one, which has been hollowed-out, lacquered and engraved with figures of scholars, ladies and plants – and a donkey. It has a wooden lid with a bone cap, carved into a wheel shape, with four spokes. It's about half as big again as a cricket ball and is in fact a container of crickets of the insect variety. I don't know how old it is but I think, since it's not of the modern factory souvenir kind, it might be of about early twentieth century vintage. This is a studio apartment in which people used to house their prized crickets during winter, adding a little lime and some millet stalks to the bottom for comfort and warmth. These things are often described as cricket 'cages' although they are more like a summer palace for crickets.

Although Lafcadio Hearn, the Greek-born Irish writer and collector of Japanese folk tales, has described cricket-keeping among the leisure pursuits of Japan, I believe it was nowhere near as widespread as in China, and the crickets were confined to singing rather than fighting, whereas Chinese crickets were also prized for their gladiatorial combat prowess. Accordingly, we might say that this, along with foot-binding, is a peculiarly Chinese pastime, going back to Tang times (618-907 CE), when ladies are said to have kept crickets, housed in little gilded cages, secreted under their pillows in order to enjoy their evening serenades. They say it's only the male crickets that sing but I have my doubts. Where is the evidence for this? Maybe it was only male crickets who thought being hidden under a lady's pillow for the night was something to sing about.

Cricket-keeping lasted well into the modern era, during which carefully-bred specimens were kept for epic cricket fights in round 'arenas' of porcelain or clay. The hobby was still attracting attention among foreigners in China as late as 1933, as is evident from an issue of *The China Journal* in my possession. This is a monthly publication, dealing with science, art, literature, travel, shooting and fishing, with editor Arthur De C. Sowerby publishing from an office in Shanghai. Among articles devoted to topics as varied as tiger hunting, botany, the birds of eastern China and the rubber-growing industry, there is a very detailed article by the editor on 'Cricket Gourds and Culture in China', complete with illustrations. Mr Sowerby begins by noting the Chinese predilection for pets of various kinds, including pigeons, to the tails of which are attached melodious whistles that sound 'like an orchestra of humming tops', but then quickly asserts that cricket-keeping takes the cake for strangeness:

But strangest of all, and one which, as far as we know, is unique amongst the peoples of the world, is the ancient and venerable custom amongst the Chinese of keeping crickets…Most people love the sound of a cricket about the hearth, but it seems to have occurred to none but the Chinese to take that little insect, put it into a suitable receptacle, tuck it away in the folds of one's clothes where it is warm and dark and feed and nurture it – all for the sake of its cheery little song! Who but the Chinese could have conceived the idea that every whit as much excitement is to be derived from watching a battle between two lusty male crickets as from a cockfight, a bullfight or even a fight between elephants, such as the Rajahs of India enjoy? And again, who but the Chinese could find sweet music in the song of the large green or black katydid as it scrapes it wings together in its little bamboo cage or ornamented gourd?

It's not only Sowerby who waxes eloquent on the business of crickets. So too does a certain Berthold Laufer (1874-1934), a German anthropologist who emigrated to the United States, worked as an assistant at the American Museum of Natural History, then as a lecturer in ethnology and East Asian Languages at Columbia University and finished a distinguished career at the Field Museum in Chicago. He was elected to the National Academy of Sciences and became president of the History of Science Society. He died in 1934 as a result of falling from the eighth-floor fire escape of a Chicago hotel. I don't know if there was a fire at the time or he'd become distracted while intent on capturing a cricket in the fire escape outside his room. He bequeathed his library and letters to the Chicago Field Museum Library, and his collection of almost four hundred wax cylinders of Chinese music recorded in 1901 and 1902, said to be the earliest sound recordings of Chinese music, went to the Indiana University Archives of Traditional Music. I can't help thinking those wax cylinders, covered with sandalwood or tortoiseshell lids, might have made excellent acoustically suitable quarters for virtuoso crickets. Perhaps that's why he collected them, thinking to provide orchestral accompaniment for the occupants.

We are indebted to Mr Laufer for his 1927 article 'Insect-musicians and Cricket Champions of China', published by the Chicago Field Museum of Natural History, Department of Anthropology, in which we learn, among other things, about the non-singing of both female and young crickets, and the practice of female cricket infanticide as a result. It's not all good news for the male of the species however, since, according to a certain Frank E. Lutz, in a 1926 article quoted by Laufer, 'the adult life of a male cricket lasts a month or so, and he chirps most of the time, but he spends little of that time in mating'. The coveted chirping sound is produced by the adult male 'raising his wing-covers above his body and then rubbing their bases together, so that the file-like veins of the under surface of the one wing-cover scrape the upper surface of the lower'. But why does he do it even when there is no female around to impress? Lutz, in his article on insect sounds, makes the rather obvious point that he may be hoping to attract one, and then goes on to say that once a male has mated 'his sexual life is done, but he keeps on chirping to his dying day'. Endearingly familiar; I see that kind of behaviour among my fellow retirees almost every day.

There is, however, an exception to vocal reticence among female crickets. According to the same Laufer article, the Chinese, with close observation of the kind that would do its author proud, although not motivated by the same love of pure science, did chance upon a species of cricket in which females rivalled males. They kept the female of the black tree-cricket, (*Homoeogryllus japonicus*), which they called the 'Golden Bell', a tribute to her tinkling melody, because she seemed to be an essential aid to male vocalisation. Laufer notes, dispassionately, 'the females of all other species are not kept by the Chinese. As soon as the insects are old enough that their sex can be determined, the females are fed to birds or sold to bird-fanciers'.

'Who but the Chinese?' asks Mr Sowerby. You can, if you search, find some sort of answer to that question, some form of non-Chinese behaviour where the detail is different but the humanity is comparable. But first you have to ask the Sowerby question – and not be too afraid of being accused of 'othering'. Deeper contemplation of curios, even cricket palaces, or the tiny slippers once worn by bound feet, allows us to recognise some of the preconceptions we bring to 'strangeness'.

3. Father Hyacinth's Map

Among the things I regard as curios are old maps. They can lead you to the strangest places. One of my favourites is an 1829 map by Father Hyacinth Bitchurin of the Russian Ecclesiastical Mission, included in his small but highly authoritative guidebook *Description of Peking* and reproduced in Juliet Bredon's own superb 1922 guidebook, *Peking*. On this map, with its host of red-numbered landmarks, you can find, in the south-western (inauspicious) section of Beijing's city walls, the *Nan Tang* (Southern Cathedral) of Matteo Ricci and Adam Schall, *Xuan Wu Men* (The Gate of Proclamation of Arms), leading from the Tartar City to the Chinese City, and the old elephant stables. These were created to house the elephants presented as tribute to the emperor by vassal states like Vietnam and Myanmar but ended up, in republican times, as the site of China's first national parliament. Perhaps somebody thought it was an ideal place for trumpeting. In imperial times the elephants were part of the city's festivals when, on Elephant Washing Day, during the hottest time of the year, a pachyderm procession emerged like carnival floats from behind Xuan Wu Men and swayed in procession down to the moat for their bath. Unfortunately, I still haven't managed to get to this place, which I believe is now part of the Xinhua Publishing compound. There are many interesting tales about the integration of the elephants into the city's life. One of my favourites is recorded by Arlington and Lewisohn in their classic *In Search of Old Peking* (1935):

> Another perquisite of the keepers was the disposing of the elephants' dung to the ladies of Peking who after washing it thoroughly used the strained-off water to wash their hair with, as it was supposed to give a brilliant gloss. It was also used by men to cure the scars which, in the days of the queue, were often exposed on the shaved crown of the head. For this reason, a slang term for persons who put on airs was *Hsiang La Ssu* [*xiang la shi*] (Elephants' Dung).

I can't help wondering, after this, if the word 'shampoo' was coined in order to distinguish it from more authentically organic sources of hair-embellishment.

South of Xuan Wu Men, the dread Gate of Death from which those condemned were led to their fate, is *Cai Shi Kou*, the old vegetable market (and execution ground) and numerous other places of interest such as *Liu Li Chang Jie*, the street of antiques and bookshops, once the site of the factory that made tiles for the imperial palaces and still a popular place for souvenirs.

In a previous book, *Redgrave's Ghost* (2019), my protagonist takes a copy of Bitchurin's map with him to the top of the Drum Tower and imagines the tiled roofs of the imperial palaces as 'the scaly hide and skeleton of a great dragon':

> From where he stood, atop the Drum Tower, within the inner 'Tartar City', his mind floated down from north to south, out along an axis of dreams, contemplating this sublime terrestrial mirror of the Vault of Heaven, from the Imperial City and Prospect Hill to the palaces and throne rooms of the Forbidden City of the North Star, out to the mighty Meridian Gate, symbol of the ancient Chinese compass, beyond the great square of Tian An Men, and on to The Gate of the Zenith Sun, its crenelated walls since torn down for ring-roads and subways, and finally to the Temple of Heaven in the 'Chinese City' with its once teeming demi-monde of temples, theatres and brothels.

Down there, outside these walls within walls, I once found another scaly hide – a hedgehog in, of all things, a hedge. Perhaps it was a portent. I also encountered one of those 'real' dragons, in the borderlands between fascination and fear.

4. The Scholar and the Beauty

京剧的魅影

For many years now I have been collecting CDs, DVDs, post-ers, postcards, playing cards, storybooks and photographs of the *yangbanxi*, the 'eight model revolutionary works' of the Cultural Revolution. These were a crucial part of the way Chinese people were taught to think about the Cultural Revolution, a way of storying 'class struggle', a form of mass ideological literacy, and a guide to keeping hold of the whip hand of proletarian virtue during factional power struggles, with diverse groups of icon-oclastic Red Guards mirroring opposing factions in the Party headquarters of the 'Forbidden City'. Membership of the mor-al-political elite was signified by zealous and conspicuous rejec-tion – hatred – of class-background impurity, whether economic or intellectual, providing a fragile and usually temporary shield against the attacks of members of a putatively purer elite. It be-came a truly vicious circle, in which, in order to stay on top you had to 'learn your lines' from the melodrama of the revolutionary operas. It may all seem alien, another world away, but substitute 'identity' for 'class' and it is not so difficult to imagine the germ of this in contemporary cultural struggles for the high ground of ideological virtue.

The works were promoted in such numbers and in so many forms, it's not unreasonable to think of their characters as Disney-like creations, or the animations created for Looney Tunes, finding their way into ubiquitous slogans, political advertisements and household items. There's a scene from one of these works that stays with me, from the story of 'The White-haired Girl' (白毛女), a ballet, an incongruously Western and elite art form in the context of Mao's isolationist and proletarian China. The scene, shown on facing page, is from a set of postcards published by the Foreign Languages Press in 1969. Xi'er, a poor peasant girl, her beautiful black hair turned white after her suffering at the hands of a traitor and landlord, forced to forage for votive food offerings in a 'haunted' temple, flies (almost literally) into a towering rage at the sight of her tormentors, who are also in hiding, fleeing from revolutionary justice. She now resembles a traditional Chinese temple ghost, and from her lair strikes fear into the heart of these cowardly scoundrels and all who would harm her. The second picture is from a black and white picture story-book version of the ballet, itself based on a Chinese folktale.

Xi'er is my favourite character of the model works, but I can't look at these pictures without being reminded of – troubled by – visits I once made to the area shown in Father Hyacinth's map, the south-western corner of the walled imperial environs of Beijing, the area dividing the 'Tartar City' from the 'Chinese City'; the netherworld

that once contained the temples, 'houses of flowers and willows', theatres, markets, and narrow, twisting, 'oblique' lanes, scenes now preserved in souvenir postcard sets with titles like 'The Charm of Old Beijing'. There I encountered phantoms of the Peking Opera.

My interest in both the revolutionary theatre and the female roles played in traditional Beijing Opera began in the 1980s. I was then meeting regularly with a Chinese friend, Wang Hsin-ping, who had lived in Beijing from the 1940s to the 1970s, in a former scholar-official family of Beijing. I had originally arranged to have Chinese conversation classes with her on Saturday mornings, but these turned into interviews and eventually, after many trips to Hsin-ping's old Beijing neighbourhood, to a book, *Tartar City Woman*, (Melbourne University Press, 1990). Among her stories was that of a famous neighbour and friend, 'The White Peony', Xun Huisheng (荀慧生), one of China's pre-revolutionary 'four great *dan*' (actors of female roles in which the character is vivacious but of lower social status). The most famous of these, the only one known in the West, a celebrated contemporary of Konstantin Stanislavski and Charlie Chaplin, was Mei Lanfang (梅兰芳). Mei Lanfang always comes up first, but I have spoken to old Chinese men who remember the coquettish, even salacious performances of Xun Huisheng as a guileful servant girl or courtesan, insisting that, as a *huadan* (花旦, 'flowery girl'), he was more alluring, more 'feminine', than any actress could hope to be. To get him and his colleagues into perspective in terms of comparable Western fame you probably have to think of Chaplin himself, or Rudolph Valentino, legends of an obsolete art, the silent movie stars. In view of Xun's later life, and events in his household, you might also think of the 1950 noir movie *Sunset Boulevard*.

The pictures on facing page show Xun in a variety of poses and costumes. His most famous role was that of Hong Niang, (红娘),

the wily and free-spirited servant girl and chamber-confidante in *The Tale of the West Wing* (西厢记, often called *Romance of the Western Chamber*), who aids her mistress to marry the poor scholar she loves instead of the rich man planned for her by mother – a classic Chinese tale of the scholar and the beauty, dating back seven centuries. Cyril Birch, the great British-American sinologist and translator, says this play may have 'delighted more people than any other play in human history'. Here is his description of the major roles from a relatively modern version of the play, in which he contrasts the characteristics of the servant girl with those of the mistress:

When our heroine first appears on the stage...this pert miss follows a mincing step or two behind her. Whether standing patiently in attendance at the side or engaging in some spirited exchange, her elfin appeal is nicely calculated to offset the tranquil beauty of her young mistress…The young lady is all demure and shrinking yet stately loveliness, concave flowing line of long gown over floor-length skirt, eyes downcast, movements a rippling shimmer accentuated by the 'water sleeves' of white silk that can droop to the floor in despair or be flung like a banner behind her head in an anguished gesture of defiance. The maid on the other hand contrasts in every detail with this kind of dignified grace. The maid is quick; she is agility personified in her silk jacket and trousers of some bright hue, selected to enliven but at the same time to intensify the more subtle elegance of the young mistress's robes. While the heroine sings, the maid stands in a respectful, attentive pose, hands clasped together and resting on her hip. But as occasion demands she can whirl round the stage, spring acrobatically at an attacker, or skilfully box the ears of an impudent serving lad. She is the sprightly complement to the young lady's serenity; vigor rather than virtue is her trademark.

As in the Elizabethan theatre men played female roles, but, during his career, as these roles opened up to women after two hundred years, Xun was generous in training aspiring young actresses in their craft. He also had a reputation as a patriot in refusing to perform for the Japanese during occupation and invested quite a lot of money in the provision of a memorial cemetery for actors in a memorial park in Beijing.

However, in May 1942, as Xun was reaching the pinnacle of his career, Mao was making a seminal speech at the Yan'an Forum on

Literature and the Arts, a speech that was to replace the 'emperors, ghosts and beauties' of the traditional stage with workers, peasants and soldiers. Mao's wife, Jiang Qing, herself a former actress in modern Western theatre, (and despised for it, among Mao's political contemporaries), seized the opportunity to turn the tables on her detractors and create a key revolutionary role for herself through the implementation of Mao's theories on art in a set of revolutionary modern operas and ballets. Xun, who had learned his craft as a boy performing in the streets, in rent-a-mourner funeral processions and temple fairs with magicians, stilt-walkers, boxers and lion-dancers, would soon be regarded as a remnant of the blood-sucking tyrants of the old feudal order. The White-haired Girl, burning with righteous indignation, would fling The White Peony from the stage, although both portrayed resourceful women victims of the old society.

Xun started life as an orphan, one of two brothers from the countryside sold in the markets of Beijing around the turn of twentieth century. He was then trained in a Hebei clapper-opera troupe, a form of training that often included not only brutal physical discipline but abuse, sadistic punishments and routine sodomisation. He escaped from the troupe with a friend, Shang Xiaoyun, also to become one of the four great *dan*, and took up with a Beijing Opera troupe, lending some of the techniques acquired in his old school; his spotlight gaze, bewitching cadences and subtle but astonishing acrobatic balance, eventually creating his own distinctive style and troupe. During the Cultural Revolution he was denounced as a representative of the 'four olds', including old culture, and died in misery, after a spell in a labour camp pulling nails out of planks, beaten with ropes and belts, and finally, after collapsing, neglected to death in hospital, quitting life, according to Hsin-ping, who was at his bedside, with a 'last flash of sunset' from those eyes that had mesmerised audiences for decades. He died on 26 December 1968, in a hospital preoccupied with celebrating Mao's birthday; Mao, who, in one of his 'three old essays' that constituted the liturgy of the Cultural Revolution, had canonised the Canadian doctor Norman Bethune for 'serving the people'. Unfortunately, the doctors in that hospital had been reassigned duties, sweeping floors and cleaning lavatories, in order to 'purify the class ranks' of bourgeois medical authorities.

In 1987 I went to Beijing with Hsin-ping, for the first of many visits to her old neighbourhood. I met Xun Linglai, the daughter of the great star, herself a Beijing opera performer and prominent person in the Beijing Opera bureaucratic scene. She, her husband Weimin and daughter (there is a cloud in her name so I will call her Jade Cloud), then about fourteen I think, were living in a large apartment in the suburbs of Beijing. Three years later, while staying at The Friendship Hotel in Beijing, I rang a number given me by Hsin-ping. Linglai's husband, Weimin, answered, rather furtively I thought, and invited me to a different address, 13 Shanxi Street, in the south-western corner of the old city, just outside the 'Tartar City' wall. I had no great difficulty finding the street, thanks to a female taxi driver who had grown up in the area, who told me proudly she was Mongolian, but on arrival nobody answered my repeated hammering on two great iron doors flanked by stone lions. I thought there must be some mistake with the street number

I had been given, or I might well have mis-heard, with Weimin's whispering. Was it *shi-san* (thirteen) or *san-shi* (thirty)? However, there was a bright new plaque on the wall, proclaiming this the former home of the famous Beijing opera star Xun Huisheng, a site now protected by the Xuan Wu District Municipal Antiquities Bureau. In view of what happened to that plaque, and the wall it was attached to, I might just as well have unscrewed it and kept it for a souvenir. At least I have the photo to remind me of several things that have vanished, including my own youth.

I thought at first the house must have been locked and left empty, but after a minute or so, looking around to see if there was some other likely house nearby, the doors creaked inward slightly and the anxious face of Weimin appeared, beckoning me inside, taking a quick look up and down the street and hastily shutting the doors behind me. He led me through a corridor of discarded cooking oil tins, bicycle wheels, bird-cages, filthy rag-mops and a scooter, to a room overlooking a ruined courtyard. Inside sat his daughter, Jade Cloud, now a beautiful young woman.

Over an odd lunch – noodles, dough-twists, and a loaf of bread and a pot of raspberry jam to make the foreigner feel at home – in the dirty and dilapidated sitting room of an old Beijing four-wing courtyard house, I learned that Linglai was dead. There had been a fire and her charred body was found in what was left of the room where we had sat and talked. But it seems she was dead before the fire started. It may have been deliberately lit to cover the traces of murder.

I know no more about the circumstances to this day, other than Hsin-ping's guarded opinion, accompanied with significant looks, that some enemies had been made in the world of Beijing Opera politics. It seems there were some in the murky theatre underworld who resented Linglai as a woman usurping a role traditionally performed by specially trained and endowed male actors who had mastered gestures, looks and movements that could only be truly appreciated by male aficionados of femininity. She was an impostor, a real female and therefore a fake female-impersonator, trading on the reputation of her famous father, rising in the ranks of theatre bureaucracy in a manner out of all proportion to her talents. Then again, my Chinese may have failed me as it grappled with powerful undercurrents and I might have misunderstood some detail or background in Weimin's hushed and rapid narration. It might also have been something to do with money, or inheritance, or a real estate issue involving crooked officials – a land deal that required demolition of both the site and its owner. Or perhaps both professional resentment and official corruption were in the mix. In any case, later that day, when I asked Jade Cloud if she was interested in following her mother and grandfather onto the stage, she vehemently rejected the idea, and there was no dissent from her father. I sensed fear in her response.

After lunch I was invited to take a look around. After picking my way through a desolate courtyard of broken tiles and grand porcelain pots sprouting long-dead weeds, followed by Weimin's feat of manipulation in springing the rusted lock on the door of the south-facing wing, I found myself in an eerie shrine to this illustrious performer whose career had spanned the era from the '30s to the '50s. It was filled with elegiac scrolls containing calligraphies by famous people; authors, artists, and politicians (including Deng Xiaoping), their tributes flapping like startled pigeons at the unaccustomed gust of air, fluttering out over an altar bearing long-decayed wax fruits and dust-encased black and white photos of the great man in his most famous roles. We passed through a doorway above which hung a painting of Xun in his celebrated role as Hong Niang, possibly a self-portrait since he was himself a keen artist.

A green panelled door gave entry to a large reception room containing grand mahogany chairs and tables cluttered with photographs. These had a dizzying impact on me as I peered into them. They seemed

to form an ever-receding tunnel, showing Xun sitting beside earlier pictures of himself sitting in this same room, same chair and same position. Beyond this was a small room containing a magnificent marble opium couch. I was beguiled but uneasy.

I gave Weimin a copy of my book, just published, which contained some photos Hsin-ping had given me, including one of Xun as Hong Niang and a rather grotesque one of Linglai in Beijing opera costume. Unlike Xun, she actually looked like a man impersonating a woman. In return Weimin gave me dozens of black and white photos of Xun in his various roles. Among them was one in which he appears as if by magic, freed from his regalia, dressed in a Western-style suit. He is a mere boy, his features both delicate and film-star handsome. His nose is long, fine and high-bridged, characteristics usually associated with foreigners, and despite the degrading experiences of his apprenticeship, he looks innocent, angelic. I couldn't help looking back and forth from this photo to Jade Cloud. That evening we ate out somewhere nearby, in a narrow and cluttered lane. I remember sudden lightning, the sky opening and the lane turning into an open drain. There were watermelons everywhere, the smell of ripe fruit mingled with Jade Cloud's gardenia scent and her luminous white face glinted in the light of street lanterns, reminding me of that photo of her grandfather as a boy and the complexion that had given him the stage name 'The White Peony'.

Just before I returned to Beijing a year later Hsin-ping received a letter from Weimin. The curse of the Beijing Opera had sought out Jade Cloud, despite her aversion to the theatre world. She had been in great danger since the fire it seems, and that house of her grandfather, to which Weimin had taken her, was intended to be a refuge, since it was listed for preservation by the Antiquities Bureau and therefore supposed to be vacant. With her mother dead, left alone with her half-crazed father in that haunted house, and threatened by the same elements that had destroyed her former privileged life, she had 'gone wild'. I can only guess exactly what form this took, but I fear she may have resorted to, or been forced into, drugs and prostitution, or at least into becoming the 'escort' of some criminal protector. In any case she had ended up in some kind of 'reform' institution or jail. It seems, no matter what she did, she was destined to descend into the demi-monde of women long portrayed in world literature and theatre, European and Chinese, from *The Lady of the Camellias* to *The Courtesan's Jewel Box*. I don't know what became of Weimin, but last I heard he had moved somewhere else, perhaps nearer the jail. I have another photo, Jade Cloud about six years old, happily practising calligraphy at home with her mother. I can't bear to think of her in that house then, and in that jail now.

On a later attempt to see what had happened to the old house, I got lost somewhere around *Xi Cao Chang Jie*, Western Pastures Street. I wondered what had once been grazed there – horses, camels, elephants? I was looking for Shanxi Street, which was very close, so I asked a man in a noodle stall for directions and was told that not only the house, but the whole street had been *chaichu le* (torn down, demolished). In those days you often saw the characters 拆除 ('For Demolition') chalked on the buildings in old lanes, the *hutong* that foreigners now love to visit, some of which remain in the tourist-frequented areas, which you can visit from a rented studio in one of the apartment blocks that have sprung up where the hutong used to be. That once-grand household of Old Peking, in which Jade Cloud and Weimin had hidden out like the ghosts of Xi'er's ruined temple, was now itself a series of grim grey apartment blocks that occupied the whole street. In fact, there was a sign on the wall of the first tower indicating that these serried ranks of blockhouses *were* Shanxi Street. I knew this sort of thing had been a regular occurrence in Beijing in recent years, but I was un-nerved by the way traces of Xun and his daughter kept disappearing.

I followed these visits with a study of the relationship between Beijing Opera and the political theatre of the Cultural Revolution, including two visits to Hsin-ping's cousin Meili, in a Warner Springs ranch, outside San Diego. She and Hsin-ping had lived in the same household in Beijing and my book had helped her glean lost information about the fate of the diasporic family that had been spread across Hawai'i, California, Japan and Australia. Eventually, some years later, she and Hsin-ping met up in Melbourne, having lost contact sometime during the Anti-Japanese War. Hsin-ping told Meili what had happened to their home, which had been re-allocated to several families. During our 1987 visit, these new residents, who had been there since the early part of the Cultural Revolution, treated us as honoured guests and allowed us to look around, Hsin-ping in silent communion with the ghosts of her childhood. Since then there's been talk of some form of compensation for loss of the old family home. As far as I know it has never eventuated but the old house was still there last time I looked in 2019, in *Toufa Hutong*, 'Hair Alley'. I thought this name might be a reference to its narrow, winding nature but Arlington and Lewisohn offer this much more interesting explanation:

Turning south along the Shun Chih Men Main Street [*Shun Zhi Men*, another name for Xuan Wu Men] we pass on our right, about half-way towards the gate, a lane with the curious name of HUMAN HAIR LANE, (*T'ou Fa Hutong*), which originates from an explosion; not one that made the hair stand on end, but that 'froze it altogether'. According to Chinese records, on the 1st day of the Fifth Moon of the 6th Year of the Ming Emperor T'ien Chi (1625) the huge arsenal north of the Elephant Stables blew up, destroying this section of the town and killing over five hundred people. The force of the explosion was said to have been such, that some women who were riding in a cart had all their clothes torn off their backs, which clothes were deposited at Ch'ang P'ing Chou, near the Ming tombs, a distance of over 25 miles. The only survivor on the actual scene of the explosion was a young lad found buried unharmed among the ruins who said that he was working with thirty men unloading kegs of powder when the explosion took place. The usual crowd having rushed to the spot and seeing a pile of what appeared to be human hair lying there, at once jumped to the conclusion that it had been blown off the heads of these men. That, at least, is how the matter is recorded in the local annals.

You can still find the lane easily enough. There's a sign pointing to the street from the main road, which used to be called *Shi Fu Ma Da Jie*, after a local scholar who won first place in the highest of the Imperial Examinations, earning himself the title of *Zhuang Yuan* (状元) and the right to marry a princess. After the revolution it was re-named *Xinhua Jie*, 'New Culture Street', but you can still find your way back into Chinese history if you buy one of the old pre-Liberation maps from the nearby curio and antiques street where once stood the factory that made tiles for the Imperial Palaces.

I briefly kept an entirely unwanted memento of my encounter with Xun's family, a brocaded silk hanging depicting '100 Sons', a traditional wedding gift wishing prodigious fertility upon the marriage of Xun Linglai and Weimin, in which scores of pig-tailed little boys are playing shuttlecock, flying kites, playing generals and fishing. It was there on the wall when I visited Linglai that first time, and was found, largely intact, after the apartment was burned down.

Weimin insisted on giving it to me, heaven knows why, a macabre gift to say the least, but he was an odd fellow – little wonder I suppose. Perhaps it mocked him, a symbol of a marriage in which he was always off-stage, with Linglai in the spotlight, inheriting her position of unwarranted and much-resented authority in Beijing's world of the arts – not even a *real* female impersonator. Perhaps life would have been different if there were sons to take some of the limelight. As for me, the picture, with its ghastly scorch marks in one corner, reminded me of a terrible irony; not only did Weimin and Linglai not have multiple sons, but their one child, a daughter, who wanted no part of her mother's world, or her grandfather's, was destined nevertheless to act out, in real life, the time-honoured role of the fallen woman.

For some time, whenever I came across the '100 Sons' as I was rummaging around among my souvenirs, I wondered what had finally become of Jade Cloud. I wish I could have saved her, helped her with a visa to Australia to stay with Hsin-ping, as I had attempted to do. Did my assurances of help, and my failed efforts, seem to her a broken promise? What was she like after her shocking experience, was she still in jail, was she even still alive? I finally threw all one hundred of those sinister little sons into a blazing log fire. This time they didn't escape the flames, and I watched their silk fibres writhe and twist until they vanished.

Below is a picture of Jade Cloud's famous grandfather in happier times, pre-Cultural Revolution, entertaining an admirer in one of those rooms I had only seen in a state of neglect, shrouded in dust and silence. I love the elegance of this old-style Chinese sitting room, but as I look at it now I get the uncanny sensation that, in intruding into that room, inserting myself into its former life, I had strayed well beyond the 'Tartar City', beyond the walls of my imaginings, out into the perilous 'Chinese City', to find myself playing a role in one of China's beloved and tragic operas about the scholar and the beauty.

5. The Fox-nymph

狐狸精

It is the animal with the big tail, a tail many yards long and like a fox's brush. How I should like to get my hands on this tail some time, but it is impossible, the animal is constantly moving about, the tail is constantly being flung this way and that…Sometimes I have the feeling that the animal is trying to tame me.
'An Animal Imagined by Kafka', *Hochzeitsvorbereitungen auf dem Lande*, (1953), in Jose Luis Borges. and Margarita Guerrero, *The Book of Imaginary Beings.*

Whenever I take my walks out into these parts of Beijing, the map I follow is made up not just with monuments, but with memories of my own and those of others, including stories. One of my favourites is *City of Lingering Splendour: A Frank Account of Old Peking's Exotic Pleasures* by John Blofeld.

Blofeld (1913-1987), was a British scholar of Chinese Buddhism and Taoism. He lived in Hong Kong and Beijing in the 1930s and travelled extensively in China from the late '30s until the Communist victory in 1949. He wrote many books, including *My Journey in Mystic China* and *The Wheel of Life* but my favourite is *City of Lingering Splendour*. Among the 'exotic pleasures' is the exquisitely painful tale of Jade Flute, a courtesan with whom he fell desperately in love, but it is his story of the *hulijing* (fox-nymph, often translated 'fox-fairy') that I number among my curios, not only because of Blofeld's account, but because of my own – I almost said 'brush' – with a contemporary version. Blofeld recounts a story told him by an American professor, Bill Luton.

This Professor Luton, while living near Tsinghua University, had heard of a student who had suddenly died, some said of tuberculosis, some said of 'uncontrolled indulgence' with a prostitute, and some said of 'a sizzling affair' conducted in a village temple with a girl who said she was a farmer's daughter. I know – that sounds like a familiar opening to a series of ribald schoolboy verses. The student, P'an, was a sickly specimen but he took on a hale and hearty appearance during this affair – temporarily. One evening he arrived early at the temple and noticed a little golden fox scurrying from the temple doorway to the altar. Then suddenly, he heard a humming sound and there was his girlfriend, standing by the altar, although he had seen nobody enter. He realised she must be a *hulijing*, a fox-nymph, so he tried to escape, but she ran towards him and flung her arms around his neck. This is how Luton, via Blofeld, tells the rest of the story, finishing, Blofeld tells us, in a mood of 'grisly solemnity'.

'After that? You know what they say about a *huliching* [hulijing]. She is irresistible. A guy who has once tasted her embrace is beyond saving. I doubt if P'an tried very hard to run away. You may know too well that a *huliching*'s ardour conceals a vampire greed for your energy; that she will suck your life from you without pity. You may realize death may come within a matter of weeks or days, but you can neither save yourself nor bring yourself to ask help from others. Every day you think "Tonight I'll go to her for the last time, and tomorrow, take the first train to Nanking – anywhere that's a hell of a distance away." But you never go. It's always tomorrow and tomorrow, until, sucked dry of the last drop of energy, you stagger or are carried home to die.'

Blofeld goes on to tell us of his affair with Jade Flute. She laughs at him for his unspoken thought that she might herself be a *hulijing*, and, while she does him no harm, leaving him only with the memory of the 'happiest night of his life', he is left spiritually unrequited. It is not Blofeld himself who withers and dies, but his passion. He had in his own words, mistaken 'swiftly withering autumn leaves for the purest gold'. That phrase, 'autumn leaves' distracts me, but first I will tell my own foxy lady tale.

A few years ago, after a pleasant day at the Drum Tower and a leisurely stroll down the east side of the Imperial City, pausing for a while in the Hall of Clocks and then crossing out to the street through the East Gate, I stood wondering how I was going to kill an hour or so before a dinner meeting with a prospective student.

A very attractive young woman approached me and asked if I was lost, a slightly different approach from the usual 'Hello, where are you from?' so I took her to be a student wanting to practise her English, which seemed pretty good, suggesting she must be enrolled somewhere in legitimate study. This, and her overall casually confident manner made me think she might have been studying overseas recently. She said she was waiting to meet her parents but had arrived too early and when I said I was myself just filling in time before a meeting she suggested we go for coffee. She led me across the road to a place that looked more like an old Beijing teahouse than any of the chic international coffee franchises and, once inside, a rather shop-worn middle-aged woman ushered us into a private room with a sofa that had seen better days – and nights. The woman's pitted peasant face reminded me of 'mapo doufu', the famous chili sauce and bean curd dish named after its legendary creator 'Pock-faced Granny'. I began to get nervous. The young woman ordered 'Dragon Well' tea and this duly appeared with some cakes and candied peanuts. I took a sip, looked anxiously at my watch and called Scarface, intending to take a photo with my dubious café companion, pay for the tea and leave. Scarface appeared but told me firmly 'no photos in here'. My friend – I will call her 'Three Fires', for reasons that will become apparent – said I could not even take *her* photo because she was a Buddhist. I have many photos of Buddhists among my souvenirs, so this only added to my growing apprehension.

We believe we have three souls and if you take a photo of a person

you steal the weakest one. I am myself quite easy to getting this

kind of effect. When I was little I was very sickening, vomit all the time for no reason, starving. My parents thought I must have a demon in me, but they listen to uncle who say they must take me to the hospital. I go twice, but nothing could be working. Then my father take me to the temple and pray and do offerings to the temple god. On the way back I am suddenly better. My father believe I must once come too close to an old woman who was barren and she was bitter and evil-hearted, so she was try to steal my spirit to be her child.

I got this by way of clarification of her multiple souls :

There are three fires in our bodies. When I am out to walk at night I never look backwards, even if I am afraid by a noise. If I look back, and there is evil spirit following me, one of my fires will leave my body through my shoulders and I will be weakened.

I assumed this was some kind of vernacular version of the Buddhist lesson on the three great fires – desire, anger and delusion – and it crossed my mind I might be in danger of all three. I wanted to get out of there so I asked for the bill, but it seemed I had to pay a kind of cancellation fee for not availing myself of the full service. The tea and peanuts amounted to seven hundred and eighty yuan, about $A156. Three Fires said it was because the Dragon Well tea was of the finest quality and the price included as much as we wanted, we could have several pots if we liked, and stay all night! For an all-night stay I suppose the tea might have proved superfluous but reasonably priced.

I was worried that if I dug in and refused to pay I might find myself arguing with a policeman who was on Scarface's payroll, so I said I would pay only five hundred. Fortunately, this worked. Three Fires, the traditional, superstitious village Buddhist, then kindly arranged an Uber cab for me on her I-phone and I left as fast as I could. I met with my student, waiting for me in a Peking Duck restaurant. I didn't tell her the story because I didn't want to appear naïve, but the incident made me realise I was nowhere near as Beijing streetwise as I thought. I couldn't help wondering though, in view of the beauty and mystery of that *hulijing*, if my embarrassment was all about naivety – or something of what Blofeld had called the 'shame of self-deception'.

This story, and my attitude to Chinese 'superstitions', may help to explain what I meant earlier when I said learning Chinese has been a kind of shamanic ordeal in which I've been broken down, dis-integrated into contending psychological forces. The language is a kind of dragon, in which the closer you get to 'the real thing', the scarier it can get. You start to examine your own behaviour and think about the different ways you can react to the same thing, depending on whether you are reacting in Chinese or in the persona moulded by your own native language and culture. You start to think again about all kinds of things you once took for granted as clear choices between right and wrong. However, this kind of ambivalence has followed me as long as I can remember, it didn't just start with China, it started with education, not just formal schooling, but with some books left in the shed at home in Port Adelaide by my uncle, an itinerant boot-maker and collector of the most wonderful of all

curios - his hard-won volumes of 'The Thinker's Library'. I can't say
I understood them at the time, but they were – fascinating. And a
little dangerous.

6. The Fox Tower

There are many stories of fox-spirits and their traditional habitats to be found in the annals of 'Old Peking'. The most well-known in the Western world is the tragic and terrible true story of Pamela Werner, the adopted, possibly White Russian orphan daughter of E.T.C. Werner, (1864-1954), a British diplomat in

China, former Consul to Fuzhou, author, ironically, of books on Chinese folklore, superstitions and myths. Her horribly mutilated corpse was found on the 8th of January 1937, in a ditch near her home, dumped among the rubbish in the remains of the canal below the 'Fox Tower', (previous page) at the south-eastern end of Beijing's Ming Dynasty city walls. She was found at about eight in the morning after Russian Orthodox Christmas, her valuable watch stopped at midnight, but not stolen. The British author Paul French, former long-term resident of Shanghai, wrote a gripping book about this called *Midnight in Peking*. Now there's a movie and you can even take an audio tour following the sites of Pamela's life and death from her nearby home to the Fox Tower. Alas, you can't walk or cycle along the wall as she might have done so many times in her pitifully short life, back and forth from the Legation Quarter to her home in 1 Armour Factory Lane. (*Kuijia Chang Hutong* 盔甲厂胡同).

The amputated south-eastern section of the Tartar City Walls, incorporating the fifteenth-century *Dong Bian Men* (Eastern Corner Gate) and the Fox Tower, twenty-nine metres high and perforated with 144 archery windows, is now part of a Ming Historical Relics Park. The tower is a highlight of these few remaining sections of the old city walls, interesting not only for their ancient Chinese history, but for modern foreign-related events, indicated by various holes punched in and around them by British railway arches and Russian cannon balls of the Boxer era. Nearby channels that were once gouged out for water by thousands of Chinese labourers are now drained or filled in. Running beside and occasionally crossing the road that takes you to Beijing's Central Station are the remains of the astonishing Grand Canal that for centuries carried boats laden with goods from Hangzhou to Beijing. Add to these changes the Communist era reconstruction carried out for roads, railway stations and subways from the '50s to the '70s and there's just enough left of Old Peking for the modern tourist imagination – if you throw in Pamela's murder.

I'm admiring the endpapers from French's book, copied from a map of Beijing drawn shortly before the terrible event. I'd love to have this map with its cartoon-style illustrations of landmarks, but it sells for thousands, so I have to make do with the Penguin endpapers. It's worth pausing from Pamela to consider the map's creator, Frank Dorn (1901-1981), a former American army Brigadier-General, an accomplished old China hand, anthropologist, novelist, painter, veteran soldier – and an interesting cook it seems. The map appears in his book *A Map and History of Peiping, with Explanatory Booklet,* (1936). I don't have this book either, but I believe he based the map on two that I do have – *In Search of Old Peking,* and *Peking,* the books referred to earlier. I've been peering into his whimsically-illustrated map, trying to get a precise sense of location.

Pamela and her father lived in a lane separated from the Fox Tower by the ditch where her body was found that morning, minus sternum and heart and drained of blood. They lived in a comfortable house with modern amenities, outside the old Legation Quarter, a foreign playground of movie-houses, clubs, hotels, skating rinks and tea-dance palaces featuring jazz bands belting out the fashionable but inauspiciously-named 'fox-trot'. Between the Legation Quarter and the old Examination Halls and paper-making district in which ancient hutongs like Armour Factory Lane were located, were the 'Badlands', an unsavoury and frequently dangerous precinct of night clubs, flophouses, opium-heroin dens and brothels, often run by stateless White Russians who had fled first to the north-eastern extremities of Russia to escape the Bolsheviks, then down into Beijing to escape the occupying Japanese. With them came many alluring and exotic women who have since become the subject of folklore, history, movies, literature and legend, countesses and ballerinas who could sing, dance, recite poetry, drop the names of illustrious acquaintances, engage in espionage, teach piano or sell their wares either as high-class courtesans or down-and-out whores.

In this mix of nations were crooked Americans (one of whom E.T.C. Werner suspected of being Pamela's murderer) and all kinds of shady British, Chinese and European opportunists and survivors. But in the more respectable parts of this south-eastern sector of the walled Tartar City lived many 'old China hands' and scholars like Werner himself, as well as diplomats and business executives, some of whom were escaping the Depression, and many of whom were Jews fleeing Nazi persecution. There were hotels and department stores, bakeries and coffee shops, like those frequented by foreigners in the famous 'Morrison Street', (see frontispiece vi) so-named by foreigners after G. E. Morrison, the Australian journalist and diplomat.

Pamela herself seems to have been something of a free spirit, cycling these parts of the city alone at night, and, it would seem, occasionally falling in with dubious company, including men who had unsavoury designs upon her. Leaving aside her terrible fate, she reminds me strongly of 'Kuniang', the waif adopted by the Italian diplomat in Daniele Vare's classic of what I like to call 'Jazz Age Peking', *The Maker of Heavenly Trousers*. On the night before she was murdered, she had, it appeared, been engaged innocently enough in ice-skating at a French venue in the Legation Quarter. To this day there is no clear-cut version of how she met with her macabre Ripper-style death, with American sex-rings and Japanese secret societies competing for attention with local superstitions about the Fox Tower. However, the Tower was not just a silent witness to these dark events but a narrative device for a tale that 'haunted the last days of Old China' as the cover of *Midnight in Peking* proclaims. It is as compelling a 'story-telling object' as you could imagine. And there above the image of the tower on the dustjacket are the embossed talons of a shadowy dragon.

A 2018 book by Graeme Sheppard, (*A Death in Peking: Who Really Killed Pamela Werner?*), suggests that, while the post-mortem, ostensibly-ritualistic dismemberment was macabre, perhaps intended as a decoy pointing to ancient Chinese cultural practice of a cannibalistic nature, the true motive for the murder was universally human and mundane. However, I will leave poor Pamela in order to return to her irascible father (known to have broken the nose of one of Pamela's admirers with his cane) and the chilling, unwittingly prophetic observation he has left in a book on my shelves, *Autumn Leaves, An Autobiography*, written nine years *before* his daughter's murder:

The history of the universe is stained, tainted, like that of a family
a member of which has committed a murder – taken a life he

cannot restore. Try to avoid it how we may, we are forced to the conclusion that the Universe is without a heart.

I've read quite a lot about the murder now, and the area in which it occurred, or at least in which the body was found, but this sentence of Werner's still haunts me more than anything to do with fox-demons or other local superstitions. And it's not just that chilling phrase 'without a heart'. Is it possible we may bring dragons and demons upon ourselves? Was Werner, in his scholarly pursuit of Chinese ghouls and goblins, the man who loved dragons? If so, he had company.

7. The Man of Smoke and Clouds

Juliet Bredon tells us that Peking is 'an old curiosity shop', the 'happy hunting ground of the collector in search of things beautiful or bizarre', in which said collector soon develops not only a habit, but a 'special mentality'. The traces and relics of Old Peking to be found in antiquarian books are such a hunting ground for me. There I can find things that spirit me away to the Legation Quarter, in the Grand Hotel des Wagons Lits, doing the foxtrot with 'a Mongolian princess, complete with oiled black hair encrusted with coral and turquoise, and arranged over a frame of what looked like horns'. This is a description from another truly fabulous book, David Kidd's *Peking Story*. Kidd (1926-1996), was an American writer, collector and connoisseur of Chinese and Japanese art, who went to Beijing in 1946 and married Aimee Yu, daughter of a former Chief Justice of the Supreme Court of China, and performer in classical Chinese opera. He left China in 1950 after the communists came to power, but wrote *All the Emperor's Horses* in 1960, revised as *Peking Story* in 1988 in which he describes this bewitching creature (who is not in costume but a real

Mongolian princess) and Bob Winter, a professor and long-term resident in Beijing, arriving at a costume party in 1949. Winter, 'a tall, amusing man and one of the oldest American residents of Peking', is dressed as Fu Manchu, a shoe-string sinister oriental moustache under his nose, accompanied by 'the legendary and often married Magdalene Grant, then still spoken of as the most beautiful woman on the China coast'. Magdalene should have been accompanied by her new husband but he, 'a Dutch businessman twice her age' had failed to materialise after their honeymoon cruise ship docked in Shanghai. It seems he had fallen overboard during the voyage and she had failed to notice.

Winter is the 'Bill Luton' who tells Blofeld the tale of the fox-nymph and the student. Paul French has also written of him in a recent on-line column called 'China Rhyming', a 'curiousity'[sic], following Blofeld's trail of a Russian émigré intersex nightclub dancer named Shura Sosnitsky, part of the fringe world Winter inhabited as a gay man himself. It's worth doing a bit of 'lingering' over Shura, described thus by Blofeld, in pronouns that transition with his prose, her bust and their gender:

Shura had been born a girl and had grown past puberty apparently quite normal. During her twelfth year her father, a Tsarist official, had been killed in the Russian Revolution, so Shura had fled her home in Tomsk and joined a party of refugees whose wanderings brought them at last to Peking. From the age of fifteen she had, like so many of her countrywomen, been compelled to earn her living as a cabaret dance-hostess; and, being exceptionally beautiful, had for several years enjoyed phenomenal success. Among her patrons – mostly Chinese officers and a few Russians who at that time still had money to spend – was a young Chinese general who actually offered to marry her. She had by then grown fond of Chinese people and willingly accepted his proposal; but, before and after her engagement, she became alarmed by the appearance of inexplicable physical changes in herself. Unhappily, these changes became so impossible to conceal that the amazed general hurriedly got himself transferred to another city; and they continued almost to the point of transforming her into a man – but not quite. According to Bill Luton, who had a reputation for uncanny knowledge of other people's secrets, Shura's exceptionally virile growth of facial hair and his well-developed feminine bust (now modestly restrained by a special garment) were not the most striking of her (now his) contradictory sex-attributes. Poor Shura, after months of grief and shame, managed to put on a cheerful expression and returned to the night-club as a male cashier.

Luton, that is, Bob Winter, diviner of people's secrets, taught Shakespeare and English literature and language for sixty years in China, from the 1920s to the 1980s. He was a student of Ezra Pound, but his many letters from Pound were destroyed by Red Guards during the Cultural Revolution. Despite placing himself in great danger during the Japanese occupation, smuggling guns and radios to anti-Japanese units outside Beijing, and his protection of revolutionary students during the Civil War, he suffered confinement and humiliation during the Cultural Revolution, but lived on until 1987. Among many tales told of him is the episode in which he smuggles documents to anti-Japanese resistance forces by taping them to his penis and wrapping the said agent of conspiracy in iodine-soaked gauze in order to deter any investigation into what appeared to be a luridly diseased organ. Not even James Bond had that ruse in the bag of tricks provided by Ian Fleming.

Winter is now buried in the Ba Bao Shan ('Eight-Treasure-Mountains') Revolutionary Cemetery in the west of Beijing, a place I have yet to get to. However, it is Bert Stern, professor at Winter's old college in Wabash, in his book *Winter in China*, (2014), who reveals the identity of Bill Luton – none other than Bob Winter, who is no better known today in China or elsewhere than Bill Luton. Stern also provides us with many fascinating insights into Winter, including the tale of the venereal-violet message-stick.

French's blog, 'China Rhyming', posted April 28th, 2022 and sub-titled 'A gallimaufry of random Chinese history and research interests', also reveals Winter's alias in the process of telling us about both Blofeld and Shura Shosnitsky/Giraldi, 'the mercurial Russian émigré intersex nightcub dance/owner'. I must say I had never laid eyes on the word 'gallimaufry' until I read E.T.C. Werner's *Autumn Leaves*, in which he describes his autobiography as such and I wonder if Paul French, like me, had never heard of the word before he read Werner and thereafter couldn't resist it. It seems a perfect place to put some traces of a man who was, in many ways, a tragic, mysterious and brilliant misfit.

One thing leads to another in this gallimaufry manner as I go from places on that map to the books on my shelves. There, in a packet between Blofeld and Kidd, is a bundle of letters from Bob Winter to my late friend Dr Ronald Price (1926-2021), a pioneer in the study of modern Chinese education, who was teaching in Beijing at the start of the Cultural Revolution. These letters are among my strangest and most precious 'curios'. Not surprisingly, I don't have letters written in the early part of the Cultural Revolution, and in fact Winter says in a letter of 18th December 1969 that 'since December 68 communications seem to have dried up'. There are large gaps in the sequence of those I do have, but these aerogrammes with their stamps and postmarks might be thought of as a Chinese scroll, bearing traces of their owners and opening out to a story, with blank spaces for the imagination.

I see today, in a review of a newly-released book, *The Wild Date Palm* (2024), that I'm not the only one entranced by these ostraca-like fragments of former lives; this antique way of inscribing the ephemeral when it was not possible to be immediate, when the space and time between the writer and the receiver had to be factored into the writing, and so many things omitted, lost. They were an art form of contradictions, of events shrunk by the constraints of time and emotions expanded by its passing – transient happenings preserved in a medium of permanence.

The author, Diane Armstrong describes getting aerogrammes from her parents, as near as I can judge, about the same time as many of the letters below were written by a forgotten person to my deceased friend:

Like the Australian pound, aerogrammes are obsolete. The young people in my family had never seen one and couldn't understand how they worked, these antediluvian handwritten missives that pre-dated emails and texts. But they were an emotional lifeline that kept people connected at a time when international phone calls were very expensive, charged by three-minute intervals and punctuated by the sound of the undersea cable.

I think, in view of this difficulty in explaining aerogrammes to people of a post-letter-writing generation, or any form of carefully-considered and lasting correspondence, such things may now qualify as curios. You have to be old enough to remember what it was like writing from overseas to someone at home, when the things you might want to ask about would cease to have any significance by the time you got a reply three weeks later – so you tried to write in a way that didn't require a response and yet still provided 'an emotional lifeline'; a style of contrived blank spaces. Now you can get an immediate response to any spontaneous thought; not sealed in an intriguing packet conveyed through the clouds, but itself a thing of clouds and lightning. Astonishing; but I wonder if an SMS message or email will ever be anybody's idea of a curio? The mystery may depend on the medium.

8. The Winter Letters

Bob Winter's type-written text, like handwriting, retains something of the writer, the physical effort and dwindling energy of an old and isolated man banging away at his typewriter, running out of room on the page, striking through his errors, all the while anticipating a delivery of new seeds, packets of hope, a contingent of fresh enterprise to lift the siege of monotony and prolong his days, new ingredients in an endless quest for the elixir of true knowledge and a productive life.

Dear Ron,

18 Dec 69

Dear Ronald,
        Your letter of October 11 came through very quick1~ ·
off writing in the flurry of activity whi~~ ~
barrassing to be in the middle ei~h···
no longer productive. My ~
to squat to weed
A.M. I ~~

8 Nov 70

Friday 13 November 69.

Dear Ronald,e
        Having been busy digging before the soil freezes too hard.

However, it's still quite warm - above 60 degrees today. I have begun Englsh-

begun to plan for next year, and having no foreign currency, I have

to depend on my friends for seeds. Can I trouble you for a few pack-

ages? I have only an old Carters catalogue for 1967, and I could use my

        Purple Podded Climbing French Beans

        Carters Crimson Ball Beetroot

        Carters Improved Early Purple Sprouting Broccoli

        Carters Early Giant Leek

        Improved Turnip-rooted Celeriac

        Carters Sunrise Tomato   and

        Thyme

        Sorry to hear that your book has been delayed. Things are

very quiet here   - only a handful of people are left in the school.

All best wishes. I often think of you.

                As ever,

The first of the letters in my possession is dated November 28, 1967. There's a gap until the second one, dated 18 December 1969. In the meantime, for three months during 1968, Winter had been held in detention after Red Guards had raided his home and destroyed his books and letters, suspecting him of being an American agent because of his connection with the Rockefeller Foundation, which had contributed to the English language project he had organised. Kidd reports, in *Peking Story*, that he was also 'chained to his bed for six months toward the end of the Cultural Revolution'.

One of the letters was written just under a year before my first trip to China in May 1975, and there's another letter dated 3 March '76, in which Winter says he is looking forward to seeing Ron in May. That was my own second trip, and my first to Beijing, in which I accompanied Ron on a La Trobe University 'foreign expert' tour. The letter triggers a memory of Ron absenting himself from one of our interminable visits to factories and communes and 'meetings' with revolutionary committees, and, on his return telling me he'd been to visit an old friend. He said he would like to have taken me along, but… and I don't remember what was said after that. It's only now, all these years later, that the weight of that missed opportunity hits me. Bert Stern, as a visiting professor at Beijing University in 1984, was more fortunate, and describes his visits to Winter on campus in an on-line article, 'One of Us', for the 2024 journal of Wabash College. Winter was in his late 90s when Stern met him. His opening remarks strike a painful chord with my own state of mind in the '70s. China had a way of making people like me feel good about ourselves to the point of not noticing what was happening to other people all around us, the very people who were making us feel good about ourselves in the first place. We were *with* them – in *their* world, away from our own world of hypocrisies, injustices and indulgences – so we thought. But we had taken our world of delusion with us. We sat above their reality on a cloud of optimism, intent on our hermetically-sealed secular pilgrimage, keen to spread the word on our return. As Stern puts it:

> It's painful for me to admit that I went to China with "Red Stars" in
> my eyes. I wanted badly to find a utopia in China of the kind that
> Mao sometimes saw himself as creating. I honestly regret the loss of

such political innocence. It was a kind of innocence that kept alive my hope for the human species. But I should have known better. Rujie's stories [a Chinese student at Stern's college] of the brutalities of the Cultural Revolution should have been enough. And there were other clues around me. But hadn't I found in the writings of the illustrious Harvard historian John Fairbank glowing pictures of Mao's China, pictures consistent with my own dreams?

In this state of ignorance I began to visit Robert Winter. I had been in China for three weeks and he had lived in China almost steadily since 1923. I was ready for a kind of discipleship. It didn't turn out as simple as that.

During and after the Cultural Revolution, the Party officially ostracized Winter. That left the 97-year-old man high and dry in a single room of his small house on the edge of the campus. Around it were scattered the ruins of his once-magnificent garden, but the man himself was confined to a rumpled cot. Though I didn't know it at the time, he was often drugged to calm the rage and other passions that otherwise could overwhelm him.

After reading Stern's recollections, I return to the letters I return to the letters in some sadness, and some regret, after reading Stern's recollections of Winter:

18 December '69

Dear Ron,

Because of my great age (84 next week) I have to take care of my diet. As vitamin supplements are not obtainable, I want to plant Carters

Hardy Green Round Turnips, for Tops, in a frame around them in February or March, so that I can start eating them as early as possible, and continue until next winter.

...I practically live on turnip tops, dandelion leaves and kale leaves. As a result, at 83 last summer I dug with my own hands my entire garden two spits deep.

July 22, 1970.

Dear Ronald

I suppose you follow the news of the Maoists in France. When the police arrested the two editors of their weekly, the **Cause of the People**, *and seized two issues, Jean-Paul Sartre courageously took up the editorship. He has been questioned by the police, but in spite of his daring them to arrest him, they have not done so. The French government has passed a law ordering the police to warn demonstrators twice to disperse, and then shoot to kill. Sartre and Geismar are planning long-term guerrilla warfare against the authorities.*

How can the universities be saved in the new society? The university as a sort of ghetto where an élite is preserved artificially as minors without responsibility must be abolished. But the children of workers and peasants must have some basis on which to build. At first they must be taught fundamental languages: their own, perhaps a foreign language or so, mathematics (which is a language), arts, sciences. Then the teaching must overlap with active life. Concrete experience of one's shortcomings in the course of working, or while engaged in research, is what drives one on to build a more coherent and deeper culture. Probably the teaching profession will also have to be abolished, that is, as a group outside society.

All teaching should proceed from knowledge or experience, not from having received a sort of title as teacher. This true knowledge can be either speculative or practical (research or social activity). In this way the curse which lies on manual labour can be progressively abolished as well as the social division of labour. But this will take time. At my age, I can hardly hope to see it in full swing. But other people certainly will…

All the seeds you so kindly sent were a great success except the beans. May was appallingly hot and dry just as they were coming up and they were scorched. Now it is raining every day, but the damage is done. One lives and learns. Best wishes,

Bob.

8 Nov 70

Dear Ronald,

It is embarrassing to be in the middle eighties and to realize that one is no longer <u>productive</u>. My knees are getting stiff and it is difficult to squat to weed, so for six months I exercise them between 4 and 5 A.M. I no longer weep with the pain but they still crack and I hope that by spring that will stop. Then I go on until 10 P.M., polish my textbook on intonation, writing in hundreds of thousands of intonation marks in Chairman Mao's works (English translation) and studying, working in the garden etc. Now that it is getting colder there is less to do in the garden and when my brain gets numb I take up my latest achievement – don't laugh! knitting. I have already become rather expert on socks and am at present doing a pair for my cook.

…In the meantime, as I said, I put off answering and yesterday your letter came (also very quickly) with the lovely view of the Rookery

where you take your walks. I don't know when you expect to leave England and I hate to bother you after all the trouble you have taken when you are so busy but as you are kind enough to offer to send me some seeds, I will give you the names of these with the understanding that if you are too busy, you will forget my request.

...I hope that you will like your new job. I have a sort of horror of Australia, although I have never been there except for a few hours in Melbourne on my way from Bombay to Los Angeles by boat in 1943.

12 March, '71

Dear Ronald,

We are kept informed in a general way about the bad behaviour of the USA government and of the opposition to it. We also hear a great deal about the hippies and escapists of all sorts.

...a parallel society is beginning to run beside the system...These rebels make no analysis, have no theory. This is, apparently, their strength and their weakness. The movement goes deep because they are free and doing what they want to do; but there is no continuity, no coherence, no theory of class struggle, except in the League of Revolutionary Black Workers (marxist-leninist) of Detroit, the only group which attempts to <u>organize</u> the workers.

...How important is all this? I have no way of knowing. The last time I was in USA was 1944. Certainly things have changed very much since then. Will these movements survive?

Perhaps the answer is to be found in a wonderful little book (170pp.) by Albert Camus (Nobel Prize '57) L'Etranger, which is the best expression I know of a universal truth: No society will tolerate a person who "does not play the game", since he "refuses to lie!' (He doesn't weep at his mother's funeral, doesn't marry, is not ambitious, doesn't regret what society calls his mistakes). He is literally an extraneous body (L'Etranger). All societies will argue that to remain healthy, they must get rid of him.

3 August '71

Dear Ronald

Australia seems to be moving towards recognition of Peking, and your work has a better chance of success.

…Work on the dictionary goes on, I have recorded a play written in English by a Chinese colleague and rehearsals have begun. In addition to works of Chairman Mao, such as <u>Yenan Talks on Literature and Art</u> which we have just read, we are planning to read or have read the <u>Communist Manifesto</u>, <u>Critique of the Gotha Programme</u>, <u>Civil War in France</u>, <u>Anti-Dühring</u>, <u>Materialism and Empirio-Criticism</u>, and <u>The State and Revolution</u>. I have just finished reading <u>Seize the Time</u>, by Bobby Seale, who has written the story of the Black Panther Party in San Francisco. Their party was formed in 1966 by Huey P. Newton, who had been stimulated apparently by reading the "Quotations from Chairman Mao". The story of their casualties in the last five years is horrifying. I have also read <u>Soul on Ice</u> by Eldridge Cleaver. Before reading these books I had only the vaguest idea of these organizations.

Thanks for the advice about the pullover. I had already been coached on the main principles of washing woollens by a German woman who lives near me. It's nice that you and Erika can have your holiday together. I hope it's not too cold in Melbourne. I have been

*swimming for two months. I don't often go to the Summer Palace,
however, because the school swimming pool is just beside my house
and I save time by swimming there.*

By the way, I don't know who Myra Roper is.[*]

3 October '71

Dear Ronald,

*…Last week a BBC medical forum confirmed what I have known for
twenty years that the reason I can swim, garden and do a full day's job
like a person one third my age is that I get enough polyunsaturated fats
(chiefly linolenic acid) and enough Vitamin E (tocopherols) to prevent
its oxidation, so that I am able to manufacture enough prostaglandins
in my body (Von Euler got the Nobel Prize in medicine last year for
this important discovery.) Now Kale is the only source of E which is
available to me, but it stops for four months in winter, during which
time I always suffer a serious decline in vigour. If it is not too expensive,
I should like to have a bottle of 50 mg. capsules to get through those
four months, as I can't get it here.*

*The dictionary progresses slowly. I've done only a few hundred entries.
There must be a full English sentence illustrating each nuance of meaning
possible to each word – hundreds of sentences for a word like "take" –
and each sentence must describe life as it appears to a future member of
communist society! The few thousand I have done have almost exhausted
my imagination. But I have learned a great deal.*

---

[*] Myra Ellen Roper AM (1911-2002) A British-born Australian educator, author and
broadcaster, Principal, University Women's College, University of Melbourne 1947-
60, 15 times visitor to China from late 1950s to 1980s, an active lobbyist for diplomatic
recognition of China and President of the Committee for Australia-China Relations.

November 3. 1972

Dear Ronald,

…Yesterday, Ida Pruitt, who is an American who is here as a guest of the government and is also an old friend of mine, came to see me. She is 84 and I shall be 86 next month. She has shrunk to a little wispy gnome, whom I would not have recognized. She declared that I look just the same as I did when we saw a good deal of each other in New York in 1943, and she took a lot of pictures of me to show my friends in the U.S. whom I haven't seen for years, as if I were a sort of freak. I swam every day this summer, as the pool is only a few steps from my house. As I was working all summer I swam from 12 to 1, and then came home for lunch.*

June 23, 1974

Dear Ronald,

I am so old that I eat almost nothing, so, during the lunch hour I go by bicycle to the Summer Palace and swim for an hour. There are two swimming pools in the university, but they are changing the water so often that most of the time they are not usable. In the winter I ride for about an hour on my bicycle. I consider this exercise absolutely vital to my health. If I stopped, I think I would get so stiff that I couldn't move. A large crowd always gathers round me in the Summer Palace, which

---

* Ida Pruitt (1888-1985), American social worker and author, born to North China Southern Baptist missionary parents and raised in a Chinese rural village, living from 1888 to 1938 in China. She was teacher and principal of Wai Ling School for Girls in Chefoo (1912-1918), the first (Rockefeller Foundation) Director of Social Service at the Peking Union Medical College and Executive Secretary of the American Committee in Support of the Chinese Industrial Cooperatives. She was an early advocate for U.S. diplomatic recognition of China and author of three classic books, *A Daughter of Han; The Autobiography of a Chinese Working Woman,* Stanford University Press, 1967; *Old Madam Yin: A Memoir of Peking Life,* Stanford University Press, 1986, and *A China Childhood,* Chinese Materials Center, 1978. She is called 'China's American daughter' in a biography of the same name (Marjorie King, The Chinese University Press, 2006).

*is converted for the moment into a circus or zoo, as the Chinese don't
expect anybody past fifty to do such things…*

*I'm so glad that you escaped the floods. Not long before you were living
here, at the end of one July it rained buckets for more than a week. I was
living alone here with a mother cat and three half-grown kittens. One
of the kittens was lost. When my garden was up to my waist in water
and had covered my bed, I put another bed on top of the first and took
refuge on it with my cat, two of the kittens, a tin of sardines and a bottle
of orange juice. After four days like that, one afternoon I saw that my
cat was listening intently and was preparing to dive into the water in my
bedroom. I couldn't hold her and she began swimming towards the front
door, which had been open for over ten days. I followed her as she swam,
my legs torn with the thorns of the rose bushes, to that little hill which
you must remember stands at my front gate. There on the top I saw a
strange sight. The missing kitten sat there crying pitifully; just beside
him on the left, sat a red weasel, and on his right, a big rat, crying in the
same way. The two of them paid no attention to me as I took my cat and
her kitten in my arms and started to wade back into my house. When
the water subsided some days later, there were six inches of mud on the
floor in which swarmed frogs, fish, one snake, and heaven knows what
else invisible to the naked eye. I often ask myself, when I remember the
scene on the hill, if three human beings in similar circumstances would
have behaved like that or whether the stronger would have started to eat
the others. A book has just come out* about a plane crash in Chili [sic]*

---

* Piers Paul Reid, 1974, *Alive: The Story of the Andes Survivors*, J.B. Lippincott Co. The
story of the Uruguayan rugby team and friends and family after Uruguayan Air Force
Flight 571 crashed in the Andes mountains on Friday October 13, 1972. Out of 45 people,
16 survived after 72 days of sub-zero temperatures.

*on the top of a mountain in which the survivors ate the livers of the dead
ones. In recent years we read of more horrors in a week than would have
been recorded in a year or more before. Do you think that the problem of
overpopulation is going to be solved that way?*

All best wishes, Bob.

Interesting that Stern describes him as being left 'high and dry'
by the Party. The watery imagery continues in the account of his
1984 visit:

> One of the first things the old man said to me after he'd roused
> himself was, "Can't you think of some way to get me out of here?"
> It was a terrible question. "Here" was not simply this house. It
> included the dead end in which a man who defined himself by
> his activity had now arrived in this house, with its slightly shady
> attendants, this terrible state of mind and body. He was like a
> great fish washed up on the shore, breathing out his last. I could
> not think of any way to get him out of there except to record his
> life, moving with him from his dead present to his vital past...
>
> ...when I later described my project to Gladys Yang*, she shook
> her head ruefully. 'You're dealing with clouds," she said...

Stern adds:

> He was a teacher, a clear thinker, a fearless man of action. That

---

was his nature. He had travelled far to find the perfect refuge, but in the end, that refuge vanished in smoke, and he was left just as alone as when he began – an outsider in Beijing as once he'd been an outsider in Crawfordsville [Indiana].

In my collection there is a hand-written letter from Gladys Yang to Ron Price, 1 August, 1975:

> *I have just received today your letter of 18 July. Your last trip sounded a mixture of pleasant and frustration – how often delegates are embarrassed by other members of their delegation. I hope this coming tour is wholly enjoyable!*[*]
>
> *We certainly hope to see you, however briefly…Bob is most difficult to contact as he still has no phone. And in fine weather you can't be sure of finding him in as he still goes swimming whenever it is fine. You can always send him a telegram, or I can do that for you if you ring me.*

Judging by his letters, Winter seems not only difficult to contact, but increasingly bitter and isolated in outlook. Eight months before this letter of Gladys Yang's he writes to Price, in a manner that reminds me strongly of E.T.C. Werner's 'A Comprehensible Theory of the Universe' in *Autumn Leaves*, written just three years after Winter left Nanjing for Beijing and Tsinghua University, cycling distance for him from where Werner and his daughter lived. I wonder if they met? Or if he'd read Werner's book?

---

[*] In fact the 1976 tour was not 'wholly' enjoyable, there were indeed embarrassments, as when our psychologist members persisted in asking about sex education in China only to be told repeatedly that all psychology was a product of bourgeois capitalist society and class structure.

20 November 74

Dear Ronald,

*The last words that Chairman Mao spoke to Edgar Snow come back to me: MO SHENG DA SAN WU FA WU TIAN.**

Man stands naked amid universal chaos and indifference. He must protect himself or perish. There is no supernatural. If you add the familiar "theory and practice" you get a simple idea which everyone (if science is to prevail in this world) will have to come to in the end. NATURE IS OBJECTIVE AND A SYSTEMATIC CONFRONTATION OF LOGIC AND EXPERIENCE IS THE SOLE SOURCE OF TRUE KNOWLEDGE. What a lot of pernicious nonsense and criminal lies the world would be spared if everybody could only accept this! Here is history as it should be taught to every child:

A Big Bang was followed by suns and planets, and on one planet which happened to be the right temperature amino and nucleic acids formed and eventually (about a thousand million years ago) the CELL had the property of dividing into two parts, each of which was EXACTLY like the parent cell. Needham [Sir Joseph Needham, British author of the stupendous 24-Volume *Science and Civilisation in China*, had met Winter in Kunming in 1942 during the Civil War between Nationalists and Communists] *tells us that the ancient Chinese Taoists had a glimmering of this, but Aristotle and all the other philosophers who formed our Western heritage were never able to get out of their heads the silly and gratuitous superstition that there was always some power OUTSIDE pulling the strings.*

---

* a play on words, in Winter's transcription from Mao's strongly Hunanese Mandarin, about a bald monk, exposed to the sun and wind, protected from the vagaries of nature only by his own fragile umbrella. Jiang Qing, Mao's wife, famously pronounced these words at her trial, meaning she stood by her deeds and defied all judgement

The following section of the letter echoes Robert Ardrey's *African Genesis*, (1961), Konrad Lorenz's *On Aggression* (1966) and the unforgettable weaponised ape of Stanley Kubrick's 1968 film *2001: A Space Odyssey*, all of which I eagerly devoured in the '70s. I was full of it, in more senses than one. And speaking of embarrassing delegation moments, I have a memory of arguing rather acrimoniously about all this with Ron, who, as a biologist himself, didn't like my popular – and amateur – palaeontology one bit. Maybe that's why he didn't take me to meet Bob in 1976. If he had taken me Bob and I might have got on like a house on fire…and ruined the friendship between him and his faithful correspondent and greengrocer.

If this had continued, we should have today nothing but these original cells. But common senses tells us that the cells must occasionally have made mistakes, and these mistakes were exactly reproduced from then on, because of INVARIANCE or NECESSITY. We now call them MUTATIONS. If they happened to FAVOUR the parents, NATURAL SELECTION caused them to be disseminated more rapidly than the cells which did not have the mutation, so in turn the vertebrate, the fish, the reptile, the bird, the ape, Peking Man, Neanderthal Man, and CRO MAGNON man were created. HA! At this point we get the explanation of what is going on in the Middle East! Cro Magnon had become so clever that he feared nothing in the world except other men. So he exterminated Neanderthal Man and GENECIDE [sic] was born. The other animals do not engage in this charming sport, only MAN enjoys it, and it got built into Man's heredity. Do you think before the sun cools man will have got it out of his system?

…NO SYSTEM OF VALUES CAN CONSTITUTE A TRUE ETHIC UNLESS IT PROPOSES AN IDEAL REACHING BEYOND THE INDIVIDUAL AND TRANSCENDING SELF TO THE POINT EVEN OF JUSTIFYING SELF-SACRIFICE, IF NEED BE. AND NO TRUE KNOWLEDGE MUST BE PUT INTO ACTION OR DISCOURSE WITHOUT THE AUTHORITY OF SUCH AN ETHIC.

And what is the purpose of all this? the reward for all this? Only its own justification.

…This is the only philosophy which I have been able to find after a very long life, which I don't feel I need to be ashamed of.

I think I know what he means by a philosophy he didn't 'need to be ashamed of'. It doesn't necessarily mean he'd found a solution to the great questions of life, but at least his purpose in living out a 'true ethic' is not based on something self-serving, like reward or salvation. He could argue its merits objectively. Winter certainly sacrificed his own safety on a number of occasions, risking his life in heroic exploits during the Anti-Japanese War and in sheltering revolutionary students after it, including an incident recounted in Stern's book, in which he hides a former student in his wardrobe to save her from the Nationalists. Did he transcend self? That may have been too much to ask, beyond those of us who harbour a self or two in our wardrobes. Winter's persistent self-hood keeps asking him, in spite of his philosophy, in spite of his upper-case cognitive certainties, if he will be rewarded, at least with a place in Chinese memory and esteem. He is, after all, a human being, although an extraordinary one – or possibly two.

February 5, 1979

Dear Ron,

...to me, Iran, Lebanon, Northern Ireland, etc, etc, etc, are going to hell because the inhabitants have been driven crazy by religion. Is it possible that Jim Jones who ordered a thousand-odd people to drink cyanide really believed that some god had ordered him to do it? It must be that people who teach all these bloody religions are all fakes who want power. It must be that what is wanted is education, understanding. I have stayed in China because they seemed to have been above such rubbish, or are they only old-fashioned and will be contaminated by the new contacts they are making? Already 92 plus, I shall never know the answer!

And finally:

20 November, 1980

Dear Ronald,

I had all sorts of bottles of minerals on my shelves. Once when I had a little pain in my knees I licked the cork of a bottle of copper sulphate which I had bought as a poison to kill insects on the undersides of vegetable leaves. The pain in my knees stopped at once. (I swear to this in spite of the fact that the BBC declared last week that arthritis is incurable.) When I found that I was taking shorter and shorter steps and by chance licked the cork of the manganese bottle I began to take longer and longer strides. And by taking small amounts of zinc and chromium I prevented cataract and am now perhaps the only person in Peking or perhaps all China who can read the smallest print that was ever made in the world from five in the morning till twelve o'clock at night.

No news except I saw Mao's wife and former first lady being marched in with a woman guard holding each elbow; all this on television.

9. Who Were You?
An Alternative Obituary

Bob Winter's letters are replete with talk of longevity and health, but paradoxically, they also reveal some confusion about his own chronological age, (detail included in my notes for this chapter). According to the obituary documented in 'Find a Grave', which I presume is derived from the Ba Bao Shan Cemetery, he didn't make it to one hundred – but the letters suggest otherwise, albeit with some confusion. Has he somehow been posthumously denied the prize, his life-long quest for the talismanic number befitting a recluse and sage? Have the trustees of the Cemetery of Eight Treasure Mountain inflicted one last unjust humiliation upon him?

Stern, who, in the words of John K. Fairbank, has 'brought Winter back into the world', describes, in *Winter in China*, what he thought at the time was a final meeting with Winter in July 1985, when he may already have been almost 100. During this meeting, Winter wanders into the past...

I told them to keep my name out of the papers. I didn't come here
on anything political. But now I'm in trouble. I wanted to be small,
so that I wouldn't be visible. But now I have become so small that
I am practically nothing.

…and returns to the recurring theme of what the Chinese think
of him. When reassured by Stern that many great people, like
Mao and Zhou Enlai think he is a good man, he replies 'Those are
just names'. Finally, he asks if they will meet again. Stern writes, 'I
hesitate. I'll be in China for three more days, but no, let it end here
because there can't be a proper end. The two of us will never be
satisfied.' Then, two years later, Stern receives a formal invitation
– to attend Winter's hundredth birthday party on December 19,
1987 (presumably not intended as the actual date, but a convenient
time for the occasion).

> Bob Winter had always longed to live to a hundred, and now,
> though having suffered every kind of deterioration, he had
> triumphed. But the birthday party itself was a kind of nightmare.
> …the ensuing ceremony was more for the guests than for Bob
> Winter. He seemed already a reluctant ghost summoned up to
> play its part in this whirlwind of living energies, but he held back,
> bewildered.

Does it matter when, or *if*, Winter had actually 'triumphed'?
Perhaps it would have mattered to him while he was alive for the
brief period following his 100th, when that magic number would

have been a powerful symbol of a life-long achievement, his pursuit of the elusive secret of long life, bestowing upon him an aura of Taoist longevity demanding reverence. Reverence…not too strong a word for the respect afforded Chinese hermits and sages, or for a man who lived so much of his life happily hidden from public gaze, other than affording the locals the spectacle of a crazy, bike-pedalling, lake-swimming, cork-licking, kale-and-turnip-tending old foreigner, yet a man tormented in the end, wondering what the Chinese might think not only of his legacy but of *him*.

That must be what he meant when dismissing the likes of Mao and Zhou Enlai as his referees; he wanted Chinese people, Chinese *culture*, to honour him, rather than receiving tributes from great political leaders and historical figures…mortals, ephemerals. Was there to be a place for him as a contributor to the immortal Chinese traditions that he loved? He had always distinguished between the notion of immanent spirit taught in Eastern philosophies and the personal, supernatural form of after-life taught in Western religions and he may have yearned for confirmation that he had become part of the spirit of China. But there was lingering doubt. Was he, in spite of his long years in China, simply a curiosity, a transient, a 'foreign friend'? I wonder if this question, or some version of it, nestles somewhere in the minds of most foreigners who go to China for long periods and for a wide variety of reasons; traveller-writers like Mary Gaunt and Isabella Bishop-Bird, scholar/adventurers like Roy Chapman Andrews and Langdon Warner, missionary doctors like A.J. Broomhall and Elliott Osgood, intermediaries and entrepreneurs, the 'Old China Hands', like George Morrison and Carl Crow, (creator of the famous and still-popular

Shanghai calendar girl ads), and the missionary women, like Mildred Cable and the French sisters, Isobel Kuhn, Henrietta Shuck, Florence Edwards and Gladys Aylward (played with romantic licence by a very Aylward-unlike Ingrid Bergman in the 1958 film *The Inn of the Sixth Happiness*, based on the 1957 biography *The Small Woman*, by Alan Burgess). And then there are those who were perhaps most conflicted of all; foreign by nature but Chinese in nurture, three truly fascinating and 'curious' women – Gladys Yang, Ida Pruitt, Pearl Buck.

Winter's letters resound with his shouted declarations on the nature of the universe, his epistemology, his didactic formulae for a variety of things from the correct teaching of languages to the correct diet for a healthy life ('all illness comes from having too much or too little of about fifty chemical substances – proteins, vitamins and minerals') and finally, in the letter of 5 February 1979, a brief and highly dubious statement of his reason for staying so long in China – its freedom from the 'rubbish' of power-seeking fakes, including cult figures inspiring religious devotion.

This is hard to reconcile with the fact that he had himself been subjected to the consequences of Party power struggles in Beijing, fostering mass hysteria among the Red Guard factions, who in turn sought to seize power from each other by means of ever-escalating demonstrations of zealotry. China had certainly not provided him with any sort of refuge from the human failings he so frequently denounces, especially the worshipping kind – the 'debilitating myths' he associates with belief in the supernatural, but which in China were applied with equal commitment to the Communist Party and its leader. He rails at any form of supernatural thinking or any notion of after-life reward as he declines with age, while at the same time attempting to reassure himself of the significance of his own life and work, of its place, not in another world, but in *his* world, China. He elevates science to the status of humanity's only hope but does so in a country that gave rise to the 'Needham question', the search for the reasons for China's centuries-long scientific and technological stagnation after a brilliant early flowering of discovery and invention. What appears like a ghost between these often-erratic lines is an intriguing blend of empirical scientist, alchemist and Taoist mystic, not unlike Needham himself.

The number 99 in his obituary seems like a cruel mockery, but there may be a lesson in it, a lesson Winter himself might have appreciated – do not make a fetish of ritual and symbolic things. He had already, in his meeting with David Kidd in 1981, demonstrated that the thing that made his life a thing of significant continuity – his memory – had succumbed to the disease of age that he had so steadfastly resisted. He had become a collection of memories in ruin, and it was the apparition of an old friendship that confronted him with this terrible reality, not in 1987, or 1985, but in 1981, the real end of this 'Peking Story'.

Kidd's description of his last meeting with 'his oldest living friend' is to me, the saddest, and most frightening, moment in a powerful, but forgotten, story:

> My time in Peking was growing short and I had yet to visit my
> old residence at the Summer Palace. Despite a dark sky and
> predictions of rain, my driver and I headed out of the city. On

the way, we would pass the former Yenching [old name for Beijing] University campus and the home of my old friend and colleague, Bob Winter. At the age of ninety-six he was my oldest living friend. A student of Ezra Pound, Bob had come to Peking in the twenties and stayed to collect Ming furniture and breed rare strains of iris. He had lived so long in China, that, after the Communist take-over, he chose to stay.

After some searching, my driver found Bob's little house. Meeting me at the door, he was old but identifiably himself and still spoke the same careful, precise English I remembered so well. He greeted me warmly, and I reminded him of the years during which we had been friends. He nodded.

'Of course I remember you,' he said and led me to a small bedroom where I took a chair while he propped himself up on his bed. To my surprise, I recognized a fifteenth-century Ming table next to the bed which Bob had always owned, and opened up, I knew, into a game board…

I had already heard that Bob had been chained to his bed for six months toward the end of the Cultural Revolution and wanted to ask if it was this bed…

…It began to rain as Bob talked on about his memories of China, his puzzling longevity, and the stern aunts who had raised him in Iowa almost a century earlier.

Later, standing in the doorway to say good-bye, he appeared so ancient I wondered that he could still be alive. He looked beyond me into the falling rain before he took my hand, squeezed it and asked, 'Who were you? Did I know you well?'

Embedded in this forlorn plea is the most terrible of questions, 'Who was I?' I don't know who Bob Winter was and I can't help him now with my speculation. My only clues are the letters, French's blog and Stern's precious tribute of a book. But one of these days I will look for him in the cemetery of Eight Treasures Mountain. I might even correct that date on his memorial if nobody is looking.

10. Strange Tales
from a Foreign Studio

I don't want to leave Winter without including something of the foreign contribution to China's 'strange tales' tradition.

Weird and quirky tales flourished in the Ming and Qing dynasties, from the sixteenth to the eighteenth centuries. The scholar-official Ling Menchu (1580-1644) for example, wrote two volumes of stories, *Slapping the Table in Amazement,* I and II. The tales, like those of his contemporary and fellow scholar-official Feng Menglong (1574-1646), were a mix of vivid imagination and biting criticism of his social milieu and Confucian conservatism. He is still quoted for the preface to his first short story collection, in which he asserts that it is much more difficult to paint a likeness of something 'real' which one has actually seen, such as a dog or horse, than to paint a ghost or goblin, a thing one has never actually seen. I have to say that doesn't seem to have stopped people painting dragons – perhaps people *do* see them.

The most famous, and most readily available in English, of what might be termed 'ghost and goblin' stories, is *Strange Tales from a Chinese Studio*, by Pu Songling (1640-1715). Even in translation these stories are 'strange' to Western readers for a variety of reasons, not just their content, but their incompleteness and sometimes downright incoherence, a hallmark of the oral tradition from which they are derived. If they appear disconcertingly weird, it's not that something has been 'lost in translation' but that something has been *retained*, something of the indigenous vernacular context and storytelling technique. In this following selection of 'strange tales from a foreign studio', non-Chinese writers have employed a Western style of presentation, but there is still more than a hint of weirdness.

Tale One: Fox–fairies at the
Bottom of the Garden

Blofeld describes his first meeting with Professor Luton, and an event every bit as strange as anything in Pu Songling.

From a tram-stop in the west city, ten minutes' walk brought us to the lane near the elephant stables where Professor Luton lived among his flowers and animals. Like my own lane, it was a typical Peking *hu-t'ung,* [hutong] with high windowless walls, broken at intervals by ornamental roofs overhanging copper-hinged gates of chipped and fading lacquer…

The gossip I had heard about Professor Luton had prepared me for some degree of eccentricity; but I was far from ready for what I saw next. A heavily built, bearded American came stalking out, a finger to his lips, making ostentatious rather than effective efforts to tiptoe silently, and carrying in his left hand a freshly severed dog's tail, raw and bloody at the end.

Blofeld and his companion are ushered into the presence of 'the greatest living master of the seven-stringed lute'. Blofeld tells us of the impact upon him:

Imposible to describe that unearthly music! It was woven of sighs and murmurs, the tinkle of jade ornaments, the wind in the pine-trees, the whispering flight of pigeons. It was ancient and remote, like ghostly music echoing faintly through the silence of a haunted grove, yet not so much melancholy as sweetly solemn with now and then a hint of gentle gaiety.

After the performance Blofeld is left alone with Luton, who, unexpectedly, instead of offering a Chinese meal, suggests ox-tail soup. Blofeld is horrified, thinking he is about to get a serve of dog's tail soup. He raises an anxious question about the impending meal and Luton invites him to take a look at his 'menagerie', which consists of various cages containing monkeys, civet cats, peacocks – and three dogs that Blofeld took to be 'Alsatians of impure stock'. He asks why they are in a cage:

Haven't you seen wolves before? No? Well these fine fellows were captured somewhere in the Manchurian forests; they are fierce enough to welcome a chance to bite your throat out…And now you shall hear what happened this morning. Just before the music started and a little while before you came, Lao Liu, my boy, came in to feed them as usual…Well, while he was still in the cage, after distributing a basket of raw meat, he went over to that trough there to turn on the water tap. Just in front of it, he saw lying on the ground a tail – a freshly bitten-off tail with blood staining the earth close to the severed end. His first reaction was to stare at each of my three wolves, looking for injuries; but, as you see, there is nothing wrong with them and their tails are all in the right place.

Blofeld surmises that another dog of some sort may have strayed too close to the cage and been sent away with no tail between his legs by the inmates, but Luton pours scorn on this idea, pointing to the tightly-meshed wire of the cage. He tells Blofeld the only explanation is the one offered by Lao Liu, which is harder to swallow than the dog-tail soup. In Lao Liu's story this tail is meant to be inexplicable, the prank of a male fox-spirit known as a *huxian* who lives in the fox-tower at the bottom of Luton's garden. These male fox-spirits are much more amenable than the female variety, and are given to disguising themselves as frolicsome old men, fond of playing pranks on the occupants of the house in which their towers are obligingly located. They are particularly adept at magic tricks consisting of impossible events leading to insoluble myteries. So there it is, the *huxian* did it. When Blofeld asks if Luton believes in such things, he simply says "Maybe 'believe' is too strong a word. Shall we say I don't entirely disbelieve."

And there is the secret of my curious-tale genre – the audience's disbelief suspended at the threshold of mystery and the canny storyteller declining to be the spoil-sport 'omniscient narrator' of the modern Western novel kind. What's more, Luton, aka Winter may have hit upon the least stressful way of reacting to the heartless universe of Werner's *Autumn Leaves*. As every day brings harrowing tales of suffering and injustice in the world, you can either resign yourself to the arbitrary and accidental nature of the cosmos or go on 'not really disbelieving' in some conscious 'string-puller' in all things, although not necessarily in the whims and caprices of the sprite who lives in the fox tower at the bottom of the garden. Some variation on the *huxian* may be as good a way of thinking of Werner's universe as any other, although they are not always benign, nor are they restricted to haunting the walled gardens of Old Peking.

Tale Two:
Skeleton Dancers and Oracles

I've written elsewhere about Joseph Rock and his association with the Shangri-La legend, in a place now part of the tourist trail in China, but I would like to include him again here as a writer of the curious tale with the aura of authenticity about it. Rock (1884-1962), was an Austrian-born American botanist, explorer, ethnologist, collector of bird and plant speciments and photographer, famous, among other things, for his exploration and documentation of minority peoples in Yunnan, Sichuan, Gansu and Qinghai (southwestern and northwestern provinces of China and eastern borderlands of Tibet). There are many interesting photos of Rock himself, including a famous one of him on horseback and wearing an outsize Davy Crockett-style fur hat, but I include one here that is more representative of his work as an ethnographer and his art as a photographer.

The photo (overleaf) was published in *National Geographic*, in a November 1928 article by Joseph Rock about the skeleton dancers of the Choni Butter Festival of Gansu (Choni is a small Tibetan autonomous principality in southwest Gansu Province, northwest China), depicting a Tibetan Buddhist ritual in which the dancers, clad in cadaver masks, imitation tiger-skin skirts and enormous claws, act as assistants to Showa the Deer, messenger of Yama, the God of Death.

Jim Goodman, researcher of ethnic minorities in northeast India, Thailand, Vietnam and southwestern China, author of two books on the study of the Naxi minority of Yunnan, and one titled *Joseph Rock and his Shangri-La*, in which the above photo appears, gives an account of the impact on Rock, who in 1926 was apparently the 'first white man' to record the possessed dancers of the Choni Butter Festival. Goodman notes that Rock was a dispassionate observer of his subjects' attitude to what might be termed the paranormal, without venturing too far into his own interpretation of such phenomena, other than to reflect on the power of suggestion among superstitious people – the power of what might be termed culturally-induced susceptibility. Nevertheless, according to Goodman, Rock was strangely affected – afflicted – by an incident at that festival:

Dressed in colorful swirling skirts over skeleton costumes, wearing masks of grinning skulls, the dancers commenced their performance…But already the stage was busy with several men holding down women in a state of wildness, who were shaking, kicking, clawing and trying to get at the dancers. The men seemed amused by what was happening, but suddenly, right in front of Rock's eyes, the men, too, appeared to be just as afflicted as the women. They also began shaking uncontrollably and had to be restrained by yet others. ..

As the dancers resumed he [Rock] was seized by a sense of powerlessness. More people succumbed to the strange, indefinable force that made them fall to the ground, shake, squirm, scream, weep and tear their clothes. Those holding them down succeeded only with their most strenuous efforts. Altogether twenty people suffered this condition duriing the dances, which were all the while continued in frenetic choreography. The sight of yet more people collapsing into this state prompted Rock's exit from the stage…

Almost as soon as Rock took a seat the powerless sensation took hold of him again. This time it was worse, for he practically lost his sight. He tried some deep breathing to try to restore himself, but it didn't seem to be working. Fearing he would collapse into a state like what he had just witnessed, he summoned the remains of his will power and left by crawling down the carpet…

As he wrote in his diary of this unprecedented experience, "It was like a filtering of something through one's body which took charge of one completely…It was the elimination of self and the control of self through another force…the lamas explain this as the god of the monastery taking possession of one's body."

However, as Goodman observes, Rock returned to the festival a year later, apparently unaffected, and the experience 'did not challenge his rationalist outlook'. It may nevertheless have influenced his ability to communicate not only the detail but any explanation of the mysterious power of such spectacles, as in the following passages from an October 1935 *National Geographic* article about the *Sungmas*, 'the living oracles of the Tibetan Church', described by Rock as roving malignant spirits who, once subdued by the spell of saintly lamas, take up residence within a host person, from which they act as oracles. The following is his description of a ritual observed in the winter of 1928 at the lamasery of Yungning in northwestern Yunnan, where a visiting Tibetan lama becomes the 'abode' of a powerful demon called Chechin. However, it seems this Chechin is not always in and the lamas have to kick up a fearful racket to let him know he is wanted back home:

Some of the lamas in attendance begin to chant the classic of Chechin, beseeching the spirit to take possession of his chu-dje [human abode]; while some ring bells or blow conch shells; and others, carrying incense burners, walk around the bowed figure of the waiting Sungma, wafting the fragrant smoke of juniper twigs as offering to Chechin…

He sat motionless on the throne in the somber chanting hall, his face buried in his hands, breathing the fragrant juniper smoke, while the deep, low tones of the chanting lamas, punctuated by bell ringing and the blowing of conch shells, lent mystery to the whole scene. A tall, curiously decorated and plumed iron hat, weighing about 50 pounds, was placed beside him…

Soon the Sungma began to accompany the lamas in their mumbling prayers, while the incense went the round, and the silent audience awaited the spirit of Chechin. Suddenly sonorous blasts of large trumpets and deafening clash of cymbals burst forth, and the Sungma moved uneasily in his seat.

A deep, gargling sound escaped him, and his hands clasped his throat. The attending lama, a brother of Balung* now lifted the huge hat upon the Sungma's head and tied it firmly under the chin. The gargling sound is believed to be a sure sign of the presence of Chechin, who, the classic relates, died by suffocating himself with a kattak, a silk scarf.

Balung still sat dreaming for a while; then all at once his body began to sway and his legs to shake. Frantically he threw himself backward while lamas held him and tried to balance him. He spat and groaned; blood oozed from his mouth and nostrils; his face became purple – inflated to such an extent that the leather chin strap burst.

He took a sword handed to him, a strong Mongolian steel

---

* The name of the Sungma's human room-to-let for Chechin

blade. In a twinkling of an eye he twisted it with his naked hands into several loops and knots!

There's much more, including the crush that occurs when, undeterred by indiscriminate flogging from the birch whips of attendants, the spectators try to partake of the blessings conferred upon the monastery's lamas by Balung in his Chechin-possessed state. But the conclusion to Rock's account is the thing I want to draw attention to, an ambivalent ending that makes this not only a fascinating story, but a curiosity, lending itself to speculation worthy of the *wunderkammer*:

> Steel swords twisted into knots by Sungmas are highly prized by Tibetans, who fasten them to doorways and above gates to temples and homes to ward off evil spirits. I have examined such swords made of excellent steel a fourth to a third of an inch thick, and found it beyond my strength to bend even the tips. Yet the Sungmas have twisted them into several spirals, beginning with the thickest parts near the hilts.
>
> That there are many fake Sungmas is evident, as is the fact that the superhuman strength and the remarkable actions of so-called genuine Sungmas are beyond the power of normal persons.

Tale Three:
Gates of Dreams

There's another tale of Lamas and Mongol-Tibetan shamanism worthy of inclusion here. Daniele Varè (1880-1956), has written a whole book of curious events, not to the taste of modern readers perhaps, but for me pure enchantment, a tale told by an Italian diplomat, son of an Italian father and Scottish mother, raised in Scotland, who served in Beijing 1908-1920. His tale, a novel, told in a mysterious fictive-autobiographical manner, concerns 'some happenings in a quiet corner of the Tartar City', namely, in my numinous south-western corner of the old city wall of Beijing, no longer there today. The happenings involve a seductive waif with a mysterious birthmark, a Mongol Abbot of dark powers, an enigmatic Russian 'great lady' called Elisalex, a diamond star called The Cross of Alexander (linked by prophecy to the fate of Russia itself), the ailing grandson of an old friend's brother – and a dog called Uncle Podger – in what is essentially a tale of dreams within dreams. The novel is called *The Maker of Heavenly Trousers*, after a tailor who lives in an apartment on the ground floor of a house near the narrator. More imporantly, Renata, known throughout the story as 'Kuniang', Mandarin for 'girl', or I think more suitably, 'lass', lives with her family on the upper floor, until, in 1908, when she is seven, her Scandinavian mother dies of typhoid and her Italian father, who is always away working for the railways, places her in the care of a convent school. That's all there is of the tailor and his heavenly trousers, but it's a marvellous title for a tale on two legs, the mundane and the magical, and it becomes a kind of honorific title for the narrator. And this author-narrator also has the knack, more than any writer of mystery I can think of except M.R. James, of distancing himself from any attempt to rely on a supernatural explanation for the inexplicable, while making the supernatural seem plausible – in the spirit of Bob Winter and the frolicsome fox spirit at the bottom of the garden, or Joseph Rock and the twisted Mongolian sword. These stories are like rubbings from dreams, escapees from the classic Chinese novel *Dream of Red Mansions*; real and not-real.

Varè's narrator, who teases us in the *Prologue* with the 'parting' remark that the patient reader may find within the book all sorts of intimate details of his life, but no mention of his name, meets the grandson of a friend's brother, who has been sent to China to wind up the estate of the friend. His name is Paul Dysart, described as 'an aristocratic and sickly young man', but the most interesting thing about him is that he has entered into a séance-like arrangement with a Mongolian abbot, Dorbon Oirad, to live his life as a dream. This abbot is, according to Paul, 'hardly human', a shamanic priest from the far north, beyond the Amur, 'very clever in inducing autohypnotic phenomena'. The narrator meets Paul in Tientsin [Tianjin] in a bazaar in aid of the Red Cross, where he agrees to buy on his behalf, at auction, an ivory cage, presumably one of those cages used by old Chinese men for 'walking' their orioles, now very collectable receptacles. They meet again next mornng for breakfast on the terrace of the Astor Hotel:

I ordered coffee and eggs at Paul's table, and then went up again to my room to fetch the ivory cage which I had bought for him the night before. Of the thousand dollars he had given me I had spent six hundred.

Paul examined his purchase with interest. It was a fine cage of beautiful ivory. The seed-box and water-trough were quite plain, but the door of the cage was made in the form of two sliding gates,which met in the middle of an opening in the bars. They were ornamented with those minute carvings which are so popular among Far Eastern peoples.

'These double gates,' said Paul, as he moved them up and down with his forefinger, 'are like the *geminae somni portae* of the Aeneid; the Gates of Sleep, which are made of horn and ivory.'

'You remind me that I too once had a classical education. *Et ego in Arcadia vixi.* If I remember rightly, the dreams that issue from the gates of horn come true, but those that pass through the gates of ivory are deceptive. Is there not something about them also in the *Odyssey?'*

'Yes. But there the twin gates are called the Gates of Dreams.'

For some moments he remained silent and absorbed, till at length I asked him what he was thinking about. He started, as if indeed awakened from a day-dream, though the veranda of the Astor House is not exactly the place for a reverie.

'I was thinking,' he said, 'that it has become almost a platitude to say that every man has more than one personality. We all try to escape from the consciously thinking self of our everyday life. Even you are not one and indivisible. Besides being yourself, you are a Maker of Heavenly Trousers.'

Falling into his mood, I answered: 'Quite right. And I put them on when I go into my study to meet the people whom I tell about in my stories. So it was with Machiavelli. When he wrote his histories he lit the candles and put on his best velvet robe to meet the great ones of the past.'

Paul smiled and added:

'We all have something to take us out of ourselves. I now have an ivory cage.'

'Which means?'

'It means that I have the dreams that the abbot gives me, and, thanks to them, a second existence. As Baudelaire would say: an artificial paradise.'

'Why call it an ivory cage?'

'Because in my other life I am suspended above the realities. And through the ivory gates of my cage pass dreams that will never come true.'

But Paul's dreams of other times, distant places and things that will never 'come true' are infused with ostensibly real or realistic events, including a ritual that is never explicitly described, something horrifying involving him, Elisalex, Kuniang and the Cross of Alexander. Energy and life itself is gradually leached away from him in the process, as in opium addiction, or possession.

Is there something of Lord Ye and the Dragon in these stories? The quirky, pointless, goblin pranks of Fate, the difficulty in distinguishing fake from real Sungmas, the debilitating visitations and recurring dreams authored by someone other than the dreamer, cages of ivory and horn... I have collected, even *loved* some of these, out of fascination, like curios. Now there's an element of fear as something 'real' emerges from those most intangible of curios – memories. In looking back over my life I see something real enough to be 'almost a platitude' and yet something not-real, fragments of a very long dream in which I have often been divided within myself, trying to settle on some kind of persona or costume, some heavenly trousers to wear in the company of others, or an ivory cage to retreat to, suspended high above realities. But I'm not alone. Far more illustrious figures than me have lived their lives behind gates of horn and ivory – including the fabled 'Hermit of Peking'.

11. Décadence Mandchoue:
The Hermit of Peking and the
Old Buddha.

In the *wunderkammer*, curios can come to a strange form of life, like the Japanese *tsukumogami*. They arise somewhere from the depths between Fact and Fiction, 'those two impostors', to echo Rudyard Kipling's famous secular sermon 'If'. In fact they are nourished with 'ifs'. For many years I have been intrigued by the strange life of uncertainties surrounding the career of Sir Edmund Trelawny Backhouse (1873-1944), a colleague in China of the previously mentioned G.E. Morrison and the writer J. O. P. Bland (1863-1945) and a contemporary in England of Oscar Wilde and Aubrey Beardsley, with whom he demonstrated far closer aesthetic affinity. He was a famed, if reclusive, resident of Beijing from 1898 until his death in 1944, a real 'Old China Hand', perhaps even 'Old China Sleight-of-Hand', involved in many shady deals with a variety of items of dubious authenticity such as imperial jewellery, literary treasures, scrolls and art

works, international shipping contracts involving fictitious mu-
nitions transported on non-existent ships and even gun-running.
In the process, however, he donated thousands of precious books
and scrolls to the Bodleian Library in Oxford, some of which are
precious and some of which are not. This is from Anne Birrell in
the *Journal of the Royal Asiatic Society* (1994):

> The Backhouse Collection in its entirety consists of about 30,000
> volumes. While it does not contain Sung [Song] editions, it is well-
> represented by Ming and Ch'ing [Qing] printed editions, and it
> constitutes a sound library of a late Ch'ing scholar. Its chief value
> lies in its 100+ Ming editions and its excellent Palace editions of
> the Ming and Ch'ing. The same cannot be said of the collection
> of about 100 scrolls, for they are usually not by the hand of the
> calligrapher they are ascribed to, but 'after' his style, such as is
> the case with a scroll in the manner of Tung Ch'i-ch'ang*. Thus,
> although Backhouse was a fraud and perpetrated numerous
> hoaxes on the world at large, and on the scholarly community, the
> reputation and standing of the collection of printed books now in
> the Bodleian is unaffected by the vagaries of the man and his own
> publications. In that sense, the letters 'Edmundus Backhouse,
> baronettus' inscribed on marble in the Bodleian remain as a
> worthy tribute to at least one of his enterprises, regardless of his
> motives and methods. Sinology is indeed indebted to Lord Dacre
> [Hugh Trevor-Roper] for his great work of historical research and
> detection. It stands as a fine example of professionalism and

---

*   Dong Qichang, Ming calligrapher and painter 1555-1636

cultured sophistication to which future practitioners should aspire.

Despite being a recluse during most of his forty-six years in Beijing, and despite his apparent aversion to 'foreigners', Backhouse engaged in a number of close and fruitful professional relationships, including services of translation and strategic advice to Morrison, and literary collaboration with Bland, with whom he wrote the works that made his name outside China – *China Under the Empress Dowager* (1910) and *Annals and Memoirs of the Court of Peking* (1914), although he later fell out with both men. Also, despite attracting the epithet 'Hermit of Peking', he did not dwell among the untrodden ways as some kind of anchorite; rather he appears to have enjoyed rare and prolonged access to the etiolated diversions of the inner sanctum of the Imperial Court. 'If he can be believed' as his biographer, Hugh Trevor-Roper, himself to become the aforesaid Baron Dacre of Glanton, says of other claims.

In *Hermit of Peking; The Hidden Life of Sir Edmund Backhouse* (1976), Trevor-Roper accuses Backhouse of forgery, of fabricating a document which he reproduces in *China Under the Empress Dowager*, a 'diary' purportedly discovered in 1900 during the Boxer Uprising (October 1899-September 1901), while he was living in the British sector, inside the Imperial City, in part of the house formerly owned by a Chinese official, Ching Shan. In making this accusation Trevor-Roper relies upon Backhouse's substantial form in fabrication of various kinds, which he describes as 'circumstantial but sufficient pooof not only that the diary of Ching-shan is a forgery but also that Backhouse himself forged it.' Ironically, Trevor-Roper, to his credit not averse to an imaginative and risk-taking style of historical narrative, was later himself ensnared in a forgery scandal in 1983, while working for *Sunday Times* when, as a director of *Times Newspapers Ltd*, he authenticated the 'Hitler Diaries', although he quickly recognised and acknowledged the mistake. Like Backhouse himself, his fame has endured more as a result of the forgery controversy than his other undeniable achievements – including the exposure of Backhouse's Ching Shan diary. Perhaps the Hermit of Peking had an ancient shamanic spell or two concealed up his elongated Chinese sleeves.

However, whether Backhouse himself did actually forge the document, and why it might have been forged in the first place if not by him, are questions that remain tantalisingly short of irrefutable proof. He did have a way of 'finding' things that worked in his favour, including a trove of recovered imperial treasures that may well have served to ingratiate him with the Empress Dowager. He claimed to have rescued these from the Summer Palace in 1900 during the Boxer Uprising in order to prevent looting by foreign troops, and to have arranged their reinstatement in the Forbidden City in 1902 after the return of the Qing court from their refuge in Xi'an. Trevor-Roper quotes Backhouse's descriptions of this venture, in which, with a party of Manchu helpers, he transports 25,000 volumes of works along with 'bronzes, jades, porcelain, ivories, paintings, calligraphy, cloisonné, lacquer, tapestries, carpets (some 600 pieces in all) to a place of safety, not my own house.' He then arranges, in May 1902, to meet with the Chief Eunuch, the infamous Li Lien-ying, to transfer the items back to the Forbidden City via a procession through the Eastern Gate. Thus is he introduced to the company of the Old Buddha, and showered with honours, including the 'First Button of official rank (jewelled not coralled)' and 'the coveted twin-eyed peacock's feather'.

As for the diary, which remained in Backhouse's possession, but did not come to light until publication of *China Under the Empress Dowager* in 1910, this is what Backhouse and Bland tell us of 'His Excellency Ching Shan' in their book (and I might add: thank goodness for Bland, who tempered Backhouse's Victorian-literati classical effusions and bewildering multilingual erudition with a bit of the writing craft):

Seen even against the lurid background of the abomination of desolation which overtook Peking in August 1900, Ching Shan's fate was unusually tragic. Above the storm and stress of battle and sudden death, of dangers from Boxers, wild Kansuh [Gansu] soldiery and barbarian invaders, the old scholar's domestic griefs, the quarrels of his women folk, his son's unfilial behaviour, strike a more poignant note than any of his country's fast pressing misfortunes. And with good cause. On the 15th of August, after the entry of the allied forces into Peking and the flight of the Empress Dowager, his wife, his senior concubine, and one of his daughters-in-law committed suicide. He survived them but a few hours, meeting death at the hands of his eldest son, En Ch'un, who pushed him down a well in his own courtyard. This son was subsequently shot by British troops for harbouring armed Boxers.

The diary was found by the translator [Backhouse] in the private study of Ching Shan's house on August 18th and saved, in the nick of time, from being burnt by a party of Sikhs. Many of the entries, which cover the period from January to August 1900, refer to trivial and uninteresting matters. The following passages are selected chiefly because of the light they throw on the Empress Dowager in that tragedy of midsummer madness – on the strong hand and statecraft of the woman, and on the unfathomable ignorance which characterises to-day the degenerate descendants of Nurhachu.[*]

The authenticity of the document had already been called into question in 1911, sixty-five years before Trevor-Roper's book, in the diary of Backhouse's former colleague G.E. Morrison, for whom he acted as translator and informant on various matters, (and whom he later denounced as the 'inquisitious and perfidious corrrespondent of the London Times'), and by William Lewisohn, co-author of *In Search of Old Peking*. Here is what Lewisohn had to say, in Beijing in 1939, while Backhouse was still around:

If I see a man walking hastily away from a body lying on the ground, my suspicions may be aroused, but I should not necessarily raise

---

* Nurhaci, 1559-1626, was founding Khan of a confederation of Jurchen tribes under the Jin Dynasty 1616-1626, precursor of the 'Manchu', or Qing Dynasty, China's last, 1644-1912. Tz'u Hsi, Yehonala, came from one of the oldest of the Manchu clans and was a descendant of Nurhaci via the marriage of the daughter of the Prince Yangkunu to Nurhaci in 1588.

the cry of "murder". But if I see him running away, covered with blood, with a pistol in one hand and a bag belonging to the victim in the other, I should certainly raise a hue and cry. It is the cumulative evidence that tells. And so it is with the question of the authenticity of this "Diary" of Ching Shan, against which there is an overwhelming tale of evidence…

Backhouse's sensitivity to these charges is evident not only in his reaction to Morrison, but in his 'Foreword to the Reader', in his memoir *Décadence Mandchou*, written 1942-3, completed thirty-three years after *Under the Empress Dowager*:

I, Sir Edmund Trelawny Backhouse, a Baronet of the United Kingdom, do hereby positively affirm on my honour and on that of my respectable family which has played a not negligible part in English public life that the studies which I have endeavoured to write for Dr. Hoeppli contain nothing but the truth, the whole truth and the absolute truth. Nothing has been added to embellish the facts, but dates, owing to the loss of my records, cannot always be accurately given, although the year or month of an official's degradation is verifiable by record; that is an event may have occurred before or later than that recorded. My intercourse with Tz'u Hsi started in 1902 and continued till her death [1908]. I had kept an unusually close record of my secret association with the empress and with others, possessing notes and messages written to me by Her Majesty; but had the misfortune to lose all these manuscripts and papers thereto relating, largely through the cowardice of my domestics and the treachery of people in whom I trusted; so that my large collection of books and documents was lost *in toto*; that is excepting for a few dictionaries and handbooks of a linguistic nature which, however, contain no notes on the (secret not to say erotic) matters wherein I have written.

Trevor-Roper went further than Morrison or Lewisohn in asserting that the Ching Shan diary was a forgery and part of a whole career of fraud and deception. His reasons for such a conclusion appear not entirely to do with the diary itself but with the manuscript of *Décadence Manchoue*, which he obviously found distasteful. Understandable I suppose. If I were to be the surprise recipient of the unpublished memoirs of Trevor-Roper, my attitude to its merits might be jaundiced by his attachment to fox-hunting and associations with Margaret Thatcher's aristocracy and Rupert Murdoch's *Sunday Times*.

Trevor-Roper's essential part in Backhouse's reputation involves Dr Reinhard Hoeppli, (mentioned in the *Foreword* above), Honorary Swiss Consul to Beijing, acting in the interests of the Allied Powers during the Japanese occupation, and a physician-friend of Backhouse. Hoeppli had commissioned the work in 1942, along with another memoir, 'The Dead Past', during a period in which he paid frequent visits to the ailing Backhouse. He edited it and produced four type-written copies for eventual distribution to the Library of the British Museum in London, the Bodleian Library in Oxford, the Bibliothèque Nationale in Paris and the Harvard College Library, Cambridge, Massachusetts. The original manuscript and first type-written copy of each of the two memoirs were, according to Hoeppli's 1946 postscript, to be given to the Bodleian Library after his death. However, in January 1973, a month before his death, Hoeppli gave the manuscripts to Dr Rudolf Geigy, a friend and colleague, the director of the Swiss Medical Institute, who, concerned at their content, passed them on to two Swiss scholars, professors of history and English literature. Both supported Hoeppli's view of the historical value of the memoirs, after which Geigy decided to pass them on to Trevor-Roper, to act as 'final arbiter'.

The Ian Fleming-like transfer of the manuscripts occurred at Basel Airport, Switzerland, in 1973, and while *Décadence* was then comprehensively discussed – and condemned as a 'pornographic novelette' – in *Hermit of Peking*, the memoirs were not published. I presume Trevor-Roper then forwarded them to the Bodleian after publication of his book in 1976. It should be noted that both Trevor-Roper and Lewisohn before him had conceded that the evidence against the truth of Backhouse's memoirs was largely, if overwhelmingly, circumstantial, and Trevor-Roper had himself noted a recollection of Hoeppli's, before he had even seen the memoirs, that an aged Manchu rickshaw-man, independent of any kind of connection with foreigners and their historical quarrels, had identified Backhouse, who happened to be passing by, as a man famous locally as the lover of T'zu Hsi.

Decades after *Hermit of Peking*, Derek Sandhaus, Shanghai-based American author, acquired the 1,393-page manuscript of

Décadence Mandchoue from the Bodleian, along with 600 pages of Dr Hoeppli's typrwritten transcription and postscript. In the *Introduction* to his edition of *Décadence,* (which includes a thousand-odd footnotes compiled by a team of language specialists) Sandhaus raises the question of whether Backhouse's baby has been thrown out with Trevor-Roper's bathwater. Hoeppli's *Postscript* to the memoirs provides guarded support for Backhouse's claims, or at least for the historical merits of the works and the deluded but genuine self-belief of their author, but Trevor-Roper considers him to have been badly taken in by his former patient. Then again, G.E. Morrison's second son Alastair (1915-2009), author of *The Bird Fancier: A Journey to Peking,* 2001, brother of Ian, the real lover of Han Suyin, portrayed as an American war-correspondent by William Holden in the 1955 movie *Love is a Many Splendored Thing,* husband of famed China photographer Hedda Hammer, collector of Chinese curios, and the person instrumental in arranging a copy of the memoirs for the Australian National University in 1974, defends his 'old friend' thus:

> I am sure it is quite mistaken to think of him as naïve. Hoeppli was
> a sophisticated intellectual. He was not taken in by Backhouse
> but despite total differences in integrity Hoeppli had enough in
> common with Backhouse to be able to sympathize with him and
> to some extent to understand him. At the same time Hoeppli was
> entertained by Backhouse's bizarre and scandalous recollections.
> They helped to enliven a very gray wartime period and Hoeppli
> recorded them with the same care as he recorded ancient or

primitive myths and beliefs about the origin of parasites. Apart from entertainment, however, he knew that the career and experiences of Backhouse were of a most extraordinary kind and I am sure that he did believe that the memoirs might contain some material of value for posterity.

It should also be noted that Hoeppli questioned the authenticity of the diary in 1946, two years after Backhouse's death, citing research conducted by Professor J.J.L. Duyvendak of the University of Leipzig.

In his *Foreword* to *Décadence* Backhouse assures his readers, emphatically, that while his memory may be at fault on occasions, there is 'no romance or embroidery' in his narrative. In fact he had an encyclopaedic memory, but, in the opinion of both Dr Hoeppli and Hugh Trevor-Roper, his fertile imagination rendered him unable to distinguish between fact and fiction. I wonder if Backhouse himself would have recognised this as a legitimate distinction? In *Décadence* he tells us that memory counts for nothing without imagination, and there is indeed something to that when it comes to literary works, but it is very hard to reconcile with his assertion that there is no romance or embroidery about his memoirs, or with the notion that there even *is* such a thing as 'the whole truth', let alone that a narrative such as his can be free of 'anything but'. In short, it may well be that Backhouse had dalliances with the Empress Dowager Tz'u Hsi and it may be that Trevor-Roper has under-rated some important evidence in support of this, but Backhouse's almost risibly salacious account of intercourse in which the dowager's prodigiously large clitoris stands in (my phrase, not his) for the 'membrum virile' (his phrase, not mine) beggars, or should I say buggers, belief. It also leads me to unworthy speculation about the title 'China Under the Empress Dowager'.

Trevor-Roper, in *Hermit of Peking*, accuses Backhouse of 'pathological obscenity', as a result of such claims in *Décadence*. They are, he says, the imaginings of a repressed homosexual, but the extent to which he was 'repressed' is a matter of some conjecture. His writing certainly isn't. The problem in judging Backhouse's veracity persists, which means, not that his works are either fact or fiction, but that it is extremely difficult to determine the proportions involved in his peculiar form of literary alchemy. Trevor-Roper himself identifies the issue with admirable clarity, describing the memoirs as – 'not merely erroneous here and there, not merely coloured by imagination in detail, but pure fantasy throughout – and yet fantasy which was spun with extraordinary ingenuity around and between true facts accurately remembered or cunningly bent to sustain it.' The 'membrum virile' is itself the stuff of a certain fantasy, a combination of European psycho-babble and Chinese folklore pertaining to dominating women, often regarded as 'castrated males'; dragon-ladies.

Fact and Fiction are the two glass doors through which to view the cabinet of curiosities that is the life of Sir Edmund Trelawny Backhouse, and both are cracked. That's why I think of him as a curio, with ample 'romance and embroidery' for the collector, albeit this amounts in his memoirs to a kind of exot-erotica, a freak show, a cabinet of carnalities, perhaps intended to shock and titillate his contemporaries in an age in which ignorance, prurience and hypocrisy were frequently brought to bear on viewing 'the yellow race'. Maybe he was just pleasuring himself. However, he was an extraordinarily ingenious entrepreneur, to say the least, phenomenally gifted in languages, including not only the Mandarin of the court but Manchu and Mongolian, and had almost certainly been introduced into inner court circles by his various pro-active interventions in the fate of looted imperial treasures. He must have seemed a very interesting curiosity indeed to Tz'u Hsi, who, by all accounts, liked both collectables and coitus.

A picture of Tz'u Hsi (hereafter, in contemporary Chinese Phonetic Alphabet, Ci Xi, 慈 禧), is reproduced as a frontispiece in *China Under the Empress Dowager* and described by the authors as a 1903 photograph of a portrait by Katharine Carl (1865-1938), American artist and author, although it appears to be simply a photograph. There is a well-known Katherine Carl portrait from this time however, one she painted for the 1904 St. Louis Exposition. In her book, *With the Empress Dowager of China* (1905), she documents life as a privileged foreigner in the imperial court during its last days. She tells us that, in painting four portraits of Ci Xi over a nine-month period, she was not allowed to use Western techniques – 'there could be no shadows and very little perspective'. The portrait referred to above shows a rather luminous Ci Xi in a jewelled shawl, with a flock of phoenixes in the background. Carl herself was not averse to looking rather regal, as in this 1905 photo from her book:

The photograph below is the one from the Bland and Backhouse book. Ci Xi, ('Auspicious Benevolence'), the 'Holy Mother', Yehonala, the former concubine, 'Old Buddha' Empress Dowager, Queen Regent of China, resplendent in her Manchu head-dress and the 'horse-shoes' mimicking her Tungusic nomad-warrior ancestors, was then sixty-eight, a year before Backhouse records that she was frolicking ingeniously with him, then thirty-two, in a 'Summer Palace Nocturne'. In the chapter of *Décadence Mandchoue* thus titled ('Summer Palace Nocturne: The Pastimes of Messalina'), he notes this age difference but seems far more concerned with the gender difference. He asks himself if he is 'sexually adequate for Her Majesty's overflowing carnality' and speculates that he would certainly not fail if 'another type of love' were in question. Ci Xi's freakish 'carnality' seems to be the product of Backhouse's own desire for a dominating homosexual partner rather than hormonal mayhem of the Shura Sosnitsky kind. Or perhaps, with his penchant for 'pathological obscenity', he chose to depict her as some kind of human hyena, a dominatrix with reversible genitalia.

In any case, Sir Edmund didn't seem to mind a bit of pain

served with his pleasures, but I do hope she was careful with those fingernails. You can see them more clearly in the 1905 portrait below, by the Dutch artist Hubert Vos (1885-1935), painted when she was 70, nearing the end of her tumultuous days. I include this because I think he has captured, in the eyes and mouth, something of the complexity of her character; a little less of the power and something of the vulnerability – and traces of the beauty and shrewdness that raised her from concubine to Empress Dowager and co-regent. She seems to be looking, not at the artist, attempting to impart an impression of the awesome power of the dragon throne, but *through* him, to her memories, perhaps to something of the life she once led as a human being, a member of a family, rather than a deity. It's my favourite picture of her. But don't mess with her. You might find yourself escorted via your elbows by a couple of sallow-faced eunuchs, to that same well in the north-eastern section of the Forbidden City where the Pearl Consort, favourite concubine of her nephew, the Guangxu emperor, (himself, with her, under house arrest in the Dowager's new Summer Palace after a short-lived attempt at reform in 1898), is said to have met her demise. According to this version of her fate, she was thrown down the well by order of Ci Xi, as a result of declining the Dowager's invitation to commit suicide rather than risk rape by foreign soldiers during the flight of the court from Beijing in 1900. Lady Pearl suggested instead that the Guangxu Emperor should stay and negotiate with the foreigners. Some say this was yet another invention of the prolific fabulist Sir Edmund Backhouse, that Ci Xi had already left

Beijing for refuge in Xi'an by the time Pearl was supposed to have been disposed of in this tidy traditional manner.

There are still many questions, many mysteries surrounding the Old Buddha. She remains, with Backhouse, somewhere between Fact and Fiction, history and legend. There is a coiled and clawed dragon in the background, none of those lady-like phoenixes of the Katharine Carl portrait. I can't see how many claws he has, probably five, symbol of the Qing emperors, the power behind the power behind the throne.

12. Celestial Theatre

If you happen one day to be doing a motorised version of the kow-tow, (叩头 *koutou*), banging your head on the back seat of a taxi, not in obeisance to the dragon throne, but in frustration, as you crawl from the airport down the Avenue of Eternal Peace towards Tian An Men and the Forbidden City, you may catch a fleeting glimpse, over to your left, of some strange objects jutting out over a dowdy grey wall; the amputated remnants of a section of the old city walls. If you are like me and the other occupants of a tour bus many years ago, as we sat fixated on the spectacle-to-come, you will remain uninformed of the significance of these until you get home and consult the great sage Sir Joseph Needham on Chinese astronomy.

On the facing page is a 1925 shot of the platform on which are mounted the instruments visible from the road (those in the background). There are others on display in the hall below, including an amazing Chinese direction-finding chariot, surely the earliest known form of vehicular GPS device. Most of the instruments shown above were built by the Flemish Jesuit astronomer and first

Director of the Beijing Observatory, Ferdinand Verbeist (1623-1688). The one in the background right is an ecliptic armillary sphere erected in 1674. Below is a picture of a fifteenth-century copy of a thirteenth-century equatorial armillary sphere designed by the Chinese hydraulic engineer and astronomer Guo Shoujing (1231-1316). This lovely instrument is located in the garden of the observatory, which contains a statue to its maker. As you can see, there are dragons supporting the sphere; it's no celestial show without dragons.

I've visited this place several times now, learnt what I can of planispheres, altazimuths and armillary spheres, struggled to understand something of their science and symbolism, admired the symmetry of meridian rings orbiting each other in a long-frozen minuet, and followed them back into their provenance of Greek, Indian, Persian, Mongol, Arab and Chinese astronomy, but I still don't understand them as I should. In a way this is a perfect example of the way curios work. They arouse unrequited curiosity, beginning with nothing more than a fleeting impression.

This place is more than a museum, it is a celestial theatre. The wall is a proscenium and behind its curtain is a pageant of ancient entities, of armillary spheres, astrolabes, quadrants and sextants, brilliant and beautiful instruments for measuring the movements of the 'celestial palaces'. They are housed in a pre-telescopic astronomical observatory, one of the oldest in the world, with its origins in thirteenth century instruments built during the Jin or Jurchen Dynasty (1115-1234) and assembled in Beijing during the Yuan (Mongol) dynasty (1279-1368), in the era of Kublai Khan. The founding Ming emperor Zhu Yuanzhang (1328-1398), transferred the instruments from Beijing to Nanjing and, during the reign of the Ming emperor Yong Le (1360-1424), copies of some of the instruments were made for Beijing.

They are suspended above the realities of modern Beijing, fragments of ancient dreams, some issuing from gates of horn, some from gates of ivory. You can find your way to them if you get the Beijing subway number one line, get out at *Jian Guo Men Nei*, and walk around behind the station. But you can easily miss it. I found this to my embarrassment one day when I got out at the required station, gazed around helplessly with a map dangling from my hand, asked an attendant which line I needed in order to proceed to the Ancient Observatory, and she, without lifting her gaze from a movie magazine, pointed behind her to – the Observatory. It is worth any amount of trouble. There you will find things far more revealing of China and its pluralistic scientific past than its affiliated showpiece Beijing Planetarium. As Sir Joseph tells us:

> Apart from the Babylonian records, so many of which are presumably wholly lost, those of the Chinese show that they were the most persistent and accurate observers of celestial phenomena anywhere in the world before the Arabs.

There is evidence of this antiquity and cultural diversity in the Mogao Caves outside Dunhuang in Gansu Province, northwestern China, on the fringe of the Gobi and Taklamakan deserts. There, in 1907, in the famous 'library cave', the Hungarian-British archaeologist Sir Aurel Stein found, or was given access to, thousands of manuscripts, paintings and calligraphies, including a Tang dynasty (618-907) 'star map', the world's oldest complete celestial 'atlas', indicating and naming hundreds of constellations and over a thousand stars (illustration on facing page). I visited the Mogao caves, including the library cave, some years ago, but in that former treasure trove, cave 17, there was only emptiness, perhaps confirmation of the Buddhist view of the ultimate nature of the universe.

The fruits of Chinese star-gazing were not, however, a matter of exclusive Han Chinese creation; seventh century Indian astronomers provided a basis on which Chinese Tantric Buddhists elaborated with their notion of infinite time and space and multi-universes,

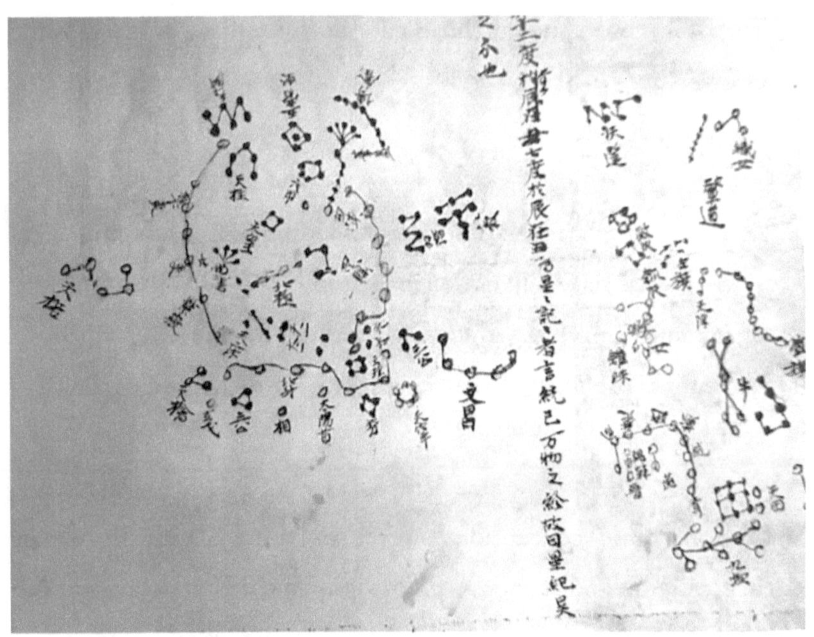

followed by Arab maritime navigators and Persian Islamic scholars, who in turn collaborated with both Chinese astronomers and European Jesuits, a process taking place over a thousand years, from the seventh to the seventeenth centuries. Long before that even, Chinese inventors contributed a hydraulic-powered armillary sphere and a seismograph for detecting the cardinal direction of earthquakes taking place hundreds of miles distant from the instrument. One of the most wonderful of these manifestations of ancient knowledge is the inscription on an oracle bone, circa 1300 BCE, the oldest known record of the appearance, and disappearance, of a nova. I can see yet, in those incisions on the bone, a handful of recognisable characters that testify to the antiquity of the script and the venerable heritage left to those of us who risk queerness in order to study Chinese. And in those cuts lie something of the cosmic order of China.

Needham again:

> Astronomy was a science of cardinal importance for the Chinese since it arose naturally out of that cosmic 'religion' , that sense of the unity and even 'ethical solidarity' of the universe, which led the philosophers of the Sung [Song] to their great organic conceptions…

These 'organic conceptions' were confronted with European science, religion and economic philosophy of the Renaissance in the guise of the Jesuit missionaries. Accurate calendars and predictions of eclipses and the movements of the planets, tracked by means of maps and devices based on a spherical earth, lent the Jesuits an air, not of spiritual authority but of shamanic powers. They were the sort of people the emperor would want to have at court, but by no means would he want them influencing the Chinese world-view, nor were they so clever that they did not actually mislead the Chinese about some aspects of the *nature* of the universe, as opposed to more efficient means of charting it. European science conveyed by Christians was based on a view of a fixed and unchanging celestial order, a universe of 'solid' matter, whereas indigenous Taoist and Sino-Buddhist Indian philosophical traditions emphasised change and fluidity, in principle closer to the insights of modern quantum physics. A superior means of mapping and measuring the movements of heavenly bodies was not in itself a means of replacing a traditional understanding of the nature – or name – of 'Heaven'.

Furthermore, as Needham points out, the part played by the Jesuits in Chinese astronomy has so many links with ancient Asian astronomy that, overall, it is unwise to emphasise Jesuit ingenuity and innovation at the expense of an appreciation of the mutual impact of Chinese and Western thought in this period. Freya Stark's words come to mind: ' we are a fellowship that looks to the same stars'. The fellowship between China and Europe was however, a fragile one, the product not just of unshared ideas but of divergent intentions, and incompatible views of political economy.

大秦景教流行中國碑

13. Shadows and Perspectives

The Chinese response to Jesuit achievements incorporated a contradiction between the efficacy of new knowledge and belief in the ultimate authority of antiquity. The Jesuits managed to produce some antiquity of their own, evidence that Christianity had a long pedigree in China, by means of the so-called Nestorian Stone, an eighth-century stone tablet of the Tang dynasty inscribed in Syriac and Chinese, documenting the 150-year old history of Christianity in China, and its recognition by the Taizong emperor in 635. The stone was buried in 845 during a period of suppression and rediscovered in 1625, the high time of the Jesuits in China.

At the top of the nine-foot stone, now in the Forest of Steles Museum in Xi'an, are the nine characters shown on the facing page, *Da Qin jing jiao bei liu xing Zhongguo bei* (Stone Commemorating the Propagation of the Luminous Teaching to China During the Great Qin (Roman Empire). The 'luminous teaching' refers to the doctrines of the Assyrian Church of the East, a western Asian schism from the Eastern Orthodox Church, associated historically rather than theologically with Nestorius, a fifth century Patriarch of Constantinople. The 'Nestorian Cross' is visible at the top. The characters *Zhong Guo* (top left) should not be read as the modern nation state of China nor in the literal sense as the 'Middle Kingdom', but as a term for the Tang state. I mention this only because people insist on believing China is different from other civilisations in thinking of itself historically as the 'centre of the world'. In fact the name denoted not the *world* but the extent of dynastic rule in the seventh century. The antiquity of the stone lent legitimacy to the mandarin status of the Jesuits and their China-provenance. They made good use of it until thwarted in what now seems a risible dispute that lasted for three hundred and fifty years, involving various emperors, popes, congregations, decrees and a whole host of Confucian sages, Catholic theologians and Enlightenment philosophers – the Chinese Rites and Names Controversy. The paragraph below, succinctly summarising a complex and protracted issue, is from Joseph Lo Bianco, *Intercultural Encounters and Deep Cultural Beliefs*, from his edited book on the English Language and China:

The Controversy is ultimately understandable only from within Western religious-politico parameters. The primary rivalry was beween religious orders, the Jesuits and Dominicans, occasionally also Franciscans, attemping to negotiate the prevailing, and shifting, Chinese worldview, as Chinese elites in turn sought to understand and respond to European intrusion. The Jesuit approach was to conduct their encounter through science, technology and cultural accommodation, an approach that changed them and their hosts, thwarted by papal denunciation of the revolutionary science of

Galileo, and eventually by papal refusal of Ricci's interpretation of the customary meaning of Chinese ancestor veneration. While most Jesuits followed the policy of syncretic accommodation, Dominican friars became agitated about the compromise it implied, eventually necessitating papal adjudication.

'Syncretic accommodation' – Needham stresses that the Jesuit contribution to Chinese science was not simply a matter of Western versus Chinese science but a matter of a universally valid *world* science taking gradual precedence over ancient and medieval forms in both civilisations. But what he calls primitive and culture-rooted forms of belief, with a distinct 'ethnic image and superscription', interrupted a period of fruitful interchange through the agency of the most ethnic of all things, a word, rooted in its parent culture, a talisman, an exclusive form of address for the supreme deity – the word for 'God', or 'Deus' and its Chinese translation. The Jesuits were content to allow Chinese Christians to use the terms *Tian* (天, 'Heaven') or *Shang Di* (上帝, 'Lord Above') as the Chinese name of 'God', while Dominicans and Franciscans were in favour of *Tian Zhu* (天主, 'Lord of Heaven'). The Jesuits were also prepared to include certain Confucian rites within the Chinese practice of Christianity. Hence, this was a 'rites and *names* controversy'.

Arguments went back and forth between meetings of the Sacred Congregation for the Propagation of the Faith during the seventeenth- century until Pope Clement XI ruled on the matter for Chinese Catholics in 1704, banning Confucian Chinese rites of 'ancestor worship' as a pagan ritual for both participants and bystanders (in fact the term is itself a misnomer, since ancestors were venerated and commemorated rather than 'worshipped'). The Jesuits considered such rituals as customs and traditions, and even argued that Europeans and Chinese had a shared history in some respects of 'civil' conduct (or universal human behaviour), but the ruling of Pope Clement XI excluded these mainstays of Chinese daily and seasonal life from the practice of Chinese Catholic Christianity. Pope Benedict XIV went further in 1742, forbidding all further debate on the issue. However, despite what seems to be their logocentric fixation, it would be doing both popes an injustice to think of them as ignorant, bigoted or even culturally insensitive men. They were scholars, patrons of great museums and libraries and preservers of antiquities, but they were looking at the issue by means of a crude theological instrument that measured words instead of ideas. Then, in 1939, Pius XII issued a decree allowing Chinese Christians to participate in Confucian ancestor commemoration. The Second Vatican Council (1962-1965), even allowed apects of Chinese ritual into Catholic liturgy.

This issue of what to call God is evident in 1907, at the Centenary Conference of the Baptist Missionary Society, as recounted in *New China, A Story of Modern Travel* (1909), by W.Y. Fullarton and C.E. Wilson, as are the divisions between Catholics and Protestants in diverse matters.

> The missions of the Roman Catholic Church, long established
> in the country, have also many adherents. Their methods are so
> different from ours that it is quite impossible for us to cooperate

in any direction, though in several instances our medical missionaries attend them in their illnesses. Friction is often caused by their practice in reference to lawsuits. Their priests have until lately been granted mandarin rank, and have claimed magisterial power. Consequently they have sought to influence the courts in favour of their members. But the Government has now ceased to recognise them in the old way, and possibly things may improve.

The authors go on to say that there are 'outstanding questions on which agreement has not yet been reached, and one of them, strange to say, is the Chinese character for the name of God'. They opine that this is a question that should be decided, 'not by the number of votes, but by the maturest knowledge'. This knowledge, in their view, ought to take account of Chinese sources, such as an unspecified ancient tablet worshipped by the Chinese on New Year's morning, which in their view refers to 'the true God who is not only worshipped by the Emperor at the Altar of Heaven, but acknowledged in the homes of the people, even though He be unknown to their hearts'. So, in their view, the Chinese had long been on the right track, even if they didn't quite know it. They add a magnanimous note, in discussing the conference, and its professed ideal of making China a Christian nation, to the effect that 'it is a worthy amibition, and although the world has never yet seen a Christian nation, that is no reason why China should not be the first'. It reminds me of that reliable old wiseacre G.K. Chesterton and his oft-quoted remark that the Christian ideal had not been tried and found wanting, but had been found difficult and left untried.

But in China there was more to religion or belief, in the broad sense, than the question of god, true or otherwise, and by whatever name. Later missionaries, Protestant and Catholic, often used the imagery of the 'Dragon and the Cross' in writing of their work, making a sharp symbolic distinction between Chinese and foreign cosmic orders. The dragon is a regular on the covers of their biographies and autobiographies, indicating something alien, a serpentine thing of heathen darkness, to be banished with the Christian symbols of light. Below, by contrast, is one of my favourites, indicating a degree of respect for the age-old and culture-transcendent mystery and power of the dragon.

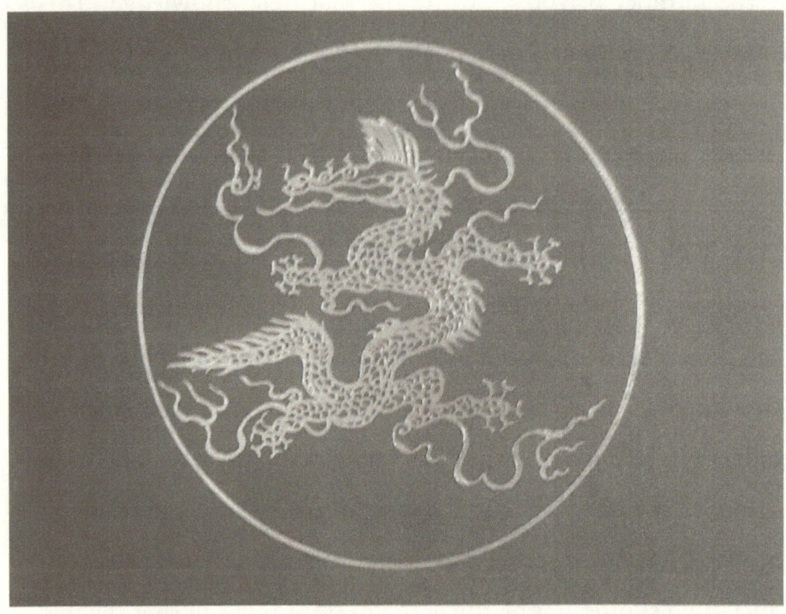

Churches these days constitute a kind of religious legation quarter for Chinese Christians. On the evening of Good Friday 2017, I witnessed a very crowded Christian quarter of the *Xuan Wu Men* district, outside one of its landmarks, the Southern Cathedral. *Nan Tang*, (南堂), the oldest Catholic church in Beijing, is a seventeenth-century baroque cathedral. The original building was a small chapel established in 1605 by the great Italian Jesuit Matteo Ricci (1552-1610) under the patronage of the Wan Li Emperor (1573-1620), who allowed him a residence and the right to conduct missionary work in Beijing. In 1650 it was expanded as a cathedral by another Jesuit, the German Johann Adam Schall von Bell (1591-1666). It was destroyed many times over the following centuries, taking its present form in 1904.

On that Good Friday evening most people, including me, were on their way to a restaurant, or out shopping, but the throng outside the church made me stop and remember; it was, almost incongruously, Easter. The Chinese term is *Fuhuo Jie* (复活节, 'coming back to life festival'). I don't know what kind of debate went into that name if any, but it's more transparent than 'Easter'. The Chinese for 'Good Friday' is *Yesu shounan jie* (耶稣受难节, 'Jesus suffering day') which is more transparent still. I joined the crowd, found my way inside and was immediately moved by traces of the dragon – and of the universal stars invoked at the beginning of Freya Stark's *Perseus in the Wind*. There was incense in the wind too, and voices of prayer and song seemed to mingle with it in a way that was familiar yet foreign, compromised yet constant. The memory remains, for me, a sublime curio, permitting vision not only into, but *between* cultures, and of forgotten intercultural pioneers.

Ricci and Bell, in addition to being missionaries and theologians, were astronomers, map-makers, instrument-makers and mathematicians, contributors to Needham's view of a 'world science' rather than a 'new science'. A later Jesuit, the Italian Giuseppe Castiglione (1688-1766), known in China as Lang Shining (郎世宁), managed to continue a tradition of intercultural curiosity, as both artist and architect – leading to works of great creativity and imagination, of shared perspectives, ending in even greater works of destruction and desolation. The need to subdue the dragon overcame admiration for it, but for a time there was hybrid beauty and mutual respect, exemplified in the paintings and architectural designs of Castiglione during his fifty-two years in China. He served three Qing emperors as a court painter, the Kang Xi, Yong Zheng and Qian Long emperors, employing a style that blended techniques from European and Chinese art, especially in the use of light, shadow and perspective, while concentrating on Chinese themes. He maintained a favoured status with the Yong Zheng emperor even during a period of the suppression of Christianity and went on to serve Qian Long for thirty years. Among his most famous works are several portraits of Qian Long, of his favourite concubine, the semi-legendary Kashgarian Muslim beauty Xiang Fei, (1734-1788, the 'Fragrant Concubine', so-called, allegedly, for her salty Western body odour), and a remarkable series on the imperial horses. On the facing page is his glorious 1739 portrait, now in the Palace Museum, Beijing, of Qian Long in ceremonial armour, coloured ink on silk, writhing dragons on breastplate:

However, in 1860, during the Second Opium War, a single, linear and limited perspective prevailed, quite unlike anything either Qian Long or Castiglione had in mind – the perspective essential for a portrait of intimidating power; all clarity, no shadows.

14. The Garden of Perfect Clarity

This is the cover for a souvenir issue pack of stamps I bought while visiting the ruins of the Old Summer Palace in Beijing some years ago, one of many visits. The illustration is an engraving of the *Hai Yan Tang Ximian*, (Western Façade, Hall of Calm Seas) an eighteeenth century Italian late baroque/rococo 'folly', part of the Western Mansions (*Xi Yang Lou* 西洋楼) which in turn form part of the *Yuan Ming Yuan*, (圆明园) 'The Gardens of Perfect Clarity' (or Brightness), a complex of imperial pleasances and seat of government for the Qing dynasty (1644-1911) for one hundred and fifty years. In the foreground are twelve bronze Chinese zodiac animals mounted on a wall flanking a fountain which featured a water-driven clock that caused the twelve animals to spout water on the hour.

The Manchu rulers, being a non-Han people from beyond the Great Wall, disliked the confines of the 'Forbidden City', preferring open spaces that reflected a self-image rooted in the traditions of nomadic warrior ancestors. From the early eighteenth century a succession of emperors ruled from what was already an elaborate network of Ming gardens, temples, lakes and waterways. The gardens were greatly expanded under Kang Xi (1654-1722), who gave them their name (suggesting a round, complete or perfect brightness, lending enlightened clarity of vision), and his successor Yong Zheng (1678-1735). The residence of the emperor encompassed an area of nine artificial islands and a lake, from which he could 'survey the world in microcosm'.

These grounds were indeed a microcosm of Chinese life, incorporating both natural features, such as hills and lakes, and a variety of outcrops of fantasy, representations of magical and supernatural realms. There were also miniature cities, toyland creations of villages and towns in which daily affairs were enacted by eunuch-actors for the pleasure of the emperor. There were shops and theatres and enactments of weddings and the proceedings of the magistrates' courts, including punishments. Yong Zheng's son, Qian

Long (1711-1799), developed the gardens to their greatest extent, covering an area of 347 hectares (857 acres, approximately eight times the size of the Vatican) and linking various areas ('scenes', including pavilions, ponds, teahouses and architectural replicas of paintings or poems), by means of over a thousand bridges. Stamps are not the only souvenir-curios one may find in the Yuan Ming Yuan shop. Below are some scenes from the gardens, depicted in a set of playing cards I bought on one visit, showing, albeit in profane and profitable form, something of the former nature and extent of the gardens.

A group of buildings in Yuanmingyuan Imperial Garden, it was named Bitongshuyuan (means study room under green phoenix trees).

A group of buildings in Yuanmingyuan Imperial Garden, it was named Louyuekaiyun (means carving moon, clouds rolled by opened).

As a result of his favoured status with Qian Long, the court painter Castiglione, in collaboration with the French engineer Michel Benoist, was entrusted with the design of an exhibition of Western curiosities to be erected inside the complex. These comprised European-style palaces and gardens, aviaries, a maze, fountains and waterworks, an outdoor theatre and various murals demonstrating *trompe-l'oeil* manipulations of perspective, all erected in the north-east corner of one of the existing gardens. These became 'The Western Palaces', halls of Western art, architecture and invention, including spectacular fountains and galleries containing many of Qian Long's impressive collection of mirrors, tapestries and clocks.

This imperial *wunderkammer*, now in ruins, is these days the site of a modern pilgrimage where young Chinese take a vow to ensure that never again will the motherland be humiliated by foreigners. It is still a place, however, of more universal contemplation, where you can sit overlooking a still, if now murky, lake, imagining the scene described by General Charles George ('Chinese') Gordon on a clear autumn day, the 12th of October, 1860:

> You can scarcely imagine the beauty and magnificence of the places we burnt. It made one's heart sore to burn them; in fact these palaces were so large, and we were so pressed for time, that we could not plunder them carefully. Quantities of gold ornaments were burned, considered as brass. It was wretchedly demoralizing work for an army. Everybody was wild for plunder. You would scarcely conceive the magnificence of this residence, or the tremendous devastation the French have committed. The throne and room were lined with ebony, carved in a marvellous way. There were huge mirrors of all shapes and kinds, clocks, watches, musical boxes with puppets on them, magnificent china of every description, heaps and heaps of silks of all colours, embroidery, and as much splendour and civilization as you would

see at Windsor; carved ivory screens, coral screens, large amounts of treasure etc. The French have smashed everything in the most wanton way. It was a scene of utter destruction which passes my description.

Among the souvenirs of this devastation was a little Pekinese dog, 'Lootie', conveyed to Queen Victoria by a certain Captain Hart Dunne of the Wiltshire Regiment. The name suggests that, unlike General Gordon, Captain Dunne was not afflicted with a sore heart.

Who ordered the destruction and why? The decision was taken by Lord Elgin, (1811-1863), aka James Bruce, Eighth Earl of Elgin, British colonial adminstrator and diplomat, former Viceroy of India and son of the Seventh Earl of Elgin, who had been instrumental in the procurement of the 'Elgin Marbles', the marble sculptures of the Parthenon. A family of looters and vandals? It may help if the linear perspective of some current historians is adjusted a little.

In the first place this lamentable event was caused by a clash of cultures with even more lasting consequences than might have followed a formal declaration of war, in particular a clash of perspectives on power and the means of demonstrating it. Britain and France were frustrated by Chinese resistance on matters of trade and diplomatic relations, and sought to exchange treaties with the Qing government during the Second Opium War (1856-1860, sometimes known as The Arrow War). The Anglo-French forces had demanded a permanent diplomatic presence in Beijing, an unthinkable barbarian presumption upon the Dragon Throne from the point of view of the Chinese. Such rights had been a vexed issue since the eighteenth century, with the failure of Lord Macartney's Mission in 1793 and Lord Amherst's in 1816, reaching a disastrous climax in the destruction of the Yuan Ming Yuan. The immediate trigger for this was the despatch to Beijing, in 1860, of a party of thirty-nine English and French negotiators and Sikh troops, in order to secure the conditions of a treaty. They were under a flag of truce but they were taken prisoner, used as hostages and tortured. Eighteen of their number died.

The allies retaliated with an attack on the Yuan Ming Yuan, which was guarded by a small force of eunuch soldiers. This is an account of the state of the prisoners from *How We Got to Pekin: The Campaign in China of 1860*, by the Reverend R. J. L. McGhee, Chaplain to the Forces. Some of the descriptions given by surviving prisoners and eye-witnesses in his book are of a kind I do not wish to include here, but this, from McGhee himself, will suffice:

> I never saw a more pitiable sight than the return of the sowars [Sikhs]; having read their own statements, you can well imagine the state of those who survived such brutal and cruel treatment. Hardly able to walk, they dragged their legs along and held their hands before their breasts in a posture denoting great suffering; and such hands as they were, crumpled up and distorted in every possible way; some with running sores at the wrists, some in which the bloated appearance caused by the cords had not yet gone away, and some were shrivelled like birds' claws and appeared to be dead and withered.

And here is his description of Elgin's retaliation:

Looking up from the entrance of the park, the groups of buildings which were scattered through the thickly wooded hollow in the hill-side extended for about a mile and a half up the hill, and reached about half-a-mile left and right of the entrance; soon after the order was given, you saw a wreath of smoke curling up through the trees that shaded a vast temple of great antiquity, which was near the centre of the park, and roofed with yellow tiles that glistened in the sun, moulded as they were in every grotesque form that only a Chinese imagination could conceive; in a few minutes other wreaths of smoke arose from half-a-hundred places…

Soon the wreath becomes a volume, a great black mass, out burst a hundred flames, the smoke obscures the sun, and temple, palace, buildings and all, hallowed by age, if age can hallow, and by beauty, if it can make sacred, are swept to destruction, with all their contents, monuments of imperial taste and luxury. A pang of sorrow seizes upon you, you cannot help it, no eye will ever again gaze upon those buildings which have been doubtless the admiration of ages, records of by-gone skill and taste, of which the world contains not the like. You have seen them once and forever, they are dead and gone, man cannot reproduce them. You turn away from the sight…

But McGhee goes on to descibe his abiding horror at the treatment of the prisoners, and concludes:

Now back again to Pekin, a good work has been done. Yes, a good work. I repeat it, though I write it with regret, with sorrow; stern and dire was the need that a blow should be struck which should be felt at the very heart's core of the Government of China, and it was done…

A man must be a poet, a painter, an historian, a virtuoso, a Chinese scholar, and I don't know how many other things besides, to give you even an idea of it, and I am not an approach to any one of them. But whenever I think of beauty and taste, of skill and antiquity, while I live, I shall see before my mind's eye some scene from those grounds, those palaces and ever regret the stern but just necessity which laid them in ashes.

Punishment, reprisal, all that…but what was the 'necessity' of this particular form? Mrs Hope Danby offers us the best clue to Elgin's motivation. I digress here in order to say I know little of Mrs Hope Danby, except that she wrote an authoritative and much-quoted book on the history of the Yuan Ming Yuan (*The Garden of Perfect Brightness*, 1950). She was also highly regarded among some notable foreign residents of Peking, including E.T.C.Werner and Charles Edward Speed Williams, Acting Commissioner of Maritime Customs, Beijing. I know that because I have seen inscriptions to her in two books, one by Werner, *Memorigrams* (The Shanghai Times, 1940) and the other *Chinese Symbolic Art* (Shanghai? 1929) by Williams. Werner, writing from the Guard Compound of the British Embassy during the Japanese occupation of Beijing, pens a poignant note to accompany the book, suggesting that he knew Mrs Danby quite well. I say 'poignant' because friendship obviously did not come easily to a man described by Jonathan Spence as 'self-insulated in a cult of loneliness' and he was still in a state of torment and anguish, three years after the shocking murder of his daughter Pamela. His notepaper contains the address, crossed out and replaced with that of the embassy compound, of his old place in Number One, Armour Factory Alley, the home he had shared with his wife Gladys until her death in 1922, and their daughter Pamela, adopted in 1919 from a Catholic orphanage near the Southern Cathedral. For me, that simple line through the old address symbolises Werner's dreadful change of fate, his violent and unforseeable eviction from domesticity into the malevolent realm of the Fox Tower. However, it is from Hope Danby's book, published ten years after Werner's note, that I gather pieces of the Lord Elgin puzzle and try to understand why it was even possible for the Reverend McGhee to consider this calamity a 'good work':

One evening five carts were seen approaching the camp; they were laden with coffins. On the 16th and 18th [October, 1860], some more coffins were sent; each was labelled with a piece of paper on which was inscribed in Chinese characters, the name of the victims translated as closely as possible by the officials. They were opened by torchlight, and it was seen that the quicklime with which they had been filled had not been sufficient to obliterate the marks of torture on the bodies.

She goes on to describe a struggle between Lord Elgin and the French envoy as to what act of reprisal should be undertaken:

The French envoy wished the punishment to descend on the Peking palaces and city, but Elgin steadfastly set his face against such a reprisal because of the innocent citizens, and the promise not to molest them that had been given by General Wolseley when he demanded the surrender of the An-ting Gate. Elgin had made up his mind that the Emperor and his officials were responsible, and therefore should be the sufferers.

Elgin sent a despatch to England, in which he explained that his notion of a suitable punishment was one that fell exclusively upon the Emperor, for whom the gardens were a favourite place. Among other reasons for his decision he cited the need to compromise between a demonstration of the destructive power of the Allies in order to frighten the Chinese into submission, and the unacceptable consequences of destroying the Forbidden City, leading to the complete collapse of the Qing government. This is Danby's description of what followed Elgin's fateful order to the British general to begin the destruction of the Yuan Ming Yuan on the 18th of October:

It was a clear autumn day, with a cloudless sky. But soon the heavens were blotted out as great columns of black clouds rose thickly in the air. The atmosphere was so still that the smoke stayed poised, like a canopy over the pleasance. Increasing with each passing moment the canopy changed to a vast black pall, heavy like that of mourning. It was such a solemn sight that witnesses spoke, with awe, of its tragic and melancholy appearance. The whole vault of the skies bespoke doom and vengeance.

After a few hours, a light wind came from the north. Slowly and gently it pushed the black mass through the air until it reached Peking. It still held pieces of burning and charred wood, and smouldering splinters and hot cinders sprinkled in the streets of the capital; ashes fell on the frightened, awe-struck people. An acrid smell of burnt paint and wood pervaded every household; it lingered for many days and nights.

Presently the weather changed in sympathy with the feelings of the Chinese. The skies were so darkened that it was as though a prolonged eclipse of the sun was taking place, and the days were shortened by it. In contrast the nights were longer; they were illumined by a red, lurid glow. Burning at first like an inferno, the conflagration gradually faded to nothing.

I took Hope Danby with me to the Yuan Ming Yuan a few years ago, an Autumn day as it happened, and sat reading her late into the afternoon, on a seat overlooking a still lake and a surviving arched bridge; a peaceful enough scene, although the atmosphere was gloomy. It wasn't just the weather, or time of day, or Mrs Danby's evocative prose, that created this lingering gloom, enabling me to imagine the scene on that dismal day in 1860. There was indeed a red, lurid glow as she describes – I know it was the result of smog and a west-returning late afternoon sun, but it made me uncomfortable, eager to get on with my visit and leave. There's a sense of unfinished business here, something else to add to awe and melancholy, something of Greek drama, of irony abroad in a vast ampitheatre of tumbled stones, another 'forest of steles', this time commemorating an undisputed foreign presence. The abiding ruins of Western palaces and follies remain to attract congregations of youth in a patriotic oath-taking ceremony, while the beautiful wooden Chinese pavilions and temples have vanished, burnt to the ground, unable to bear witness.

So it is that relics of Western architecture – and perspective – have survived to facilitate ritual condemnation of the act Victor Hugo condemned as barbarism, and of the civilisation that inspired their construction. Hugo's words are inscribed here in the ruins; how could nations that called themselves civilised, that considered themselves superior, commit such an atrocity? I recall translating the French for some Chinese tourists from Guizhou, who were very grateful and appreciative – so much so they were pleased to escort me back to the front gate an hour later when they found me scratching my head, wondering where I was. I was in turn grateful, I didn't want to spend the night, or even dusk, in that blighted and haunted place. Another irony; while Elgin calculated that the destruction of the Summer Palace would provide a limited demonstration of Western power, thus enabling the Chinese to forget relatively quickly – especially since these playgrounds were the privilege of feudal autocrats – the ruins have been turned by proletarian successors of empire into a powerful monument, a shrine, and call to arms, for the redress of China's 100 year humiliation. The cards on facing page show two symbols of this temple of eloquent ruins, *Da Shui Fa*, (The Great Fountain), and the more recent 'National Humiliation Wall'.

There are different ways of interpreting both the creation and destruction of the Yuan Ming Yuan. The pleasances of the Western

The ruin of Dashuifa (the Grand Fountain), a fountain with European style, is the most symbolist scene in Yuanmingyuan Park.

The National Humiliation Wall, was build in 1997, which commemorates how the Yuanmingyuan Park destroyed by foreign invaders.

Palaces were, like Castiglione's paintings, a combination of Western techniques and Chinese themes. Beyond the Western difference was an over-arching principle – that whatever perspective was employed in viewing, all things took meaning from their place within a Chinese cosmology. This is succinctly explained as a form of spectacle in *China on Paper: European and Chinese Works from the Late Sixteenth to the Early Nineteenth Century*, (2007):

Despite the harmonious architectural blend, the complex offered an exotic experience because of the way it was intended to function: it was designed as a series of stage sets, most of which the Qianlong emperor was supposed to view frontally in order to experience the power of linear perspective to pull the viewer into the illusion of a totalizing reality. When transmitting European geometry and linear perspective to China, the missionaries employed an accommodationist strategy whereby their basic principles were shown to demonstrate existing Chinese cosmological and artistic concepts.

What Western cosmological principle was evident in the spectacle of the Yuan Ming Yuan laid waste? Lord Elgin juggled several notions in his head, but sheer vandalism and looting as a form of reprisal was not one of them. Among other things he calculated that it was the emperor who should be punished, not the people, so he took his anger out on the imperial playground. This also obviated a direct attack on the Forbidden City, which might have precipitated the complete collapse of the Qing government and resultant chaos, hardly conducive to trade. He was also persuaded that this destruction would produce the necessary lesson and warning without the permanent enmity that would result from further incursion into the city; he could not foresee that these stone relics would be made to live on in Chinese national memory, to become a form of theatrical pedagogy. Technique and perspective have been blended again in a visual display, but these days the perspective is Chinese.

After the conflagration many wonderful things came to rest in cabinets of curiosities scattered across the world, in 47 museums listed by UNESCO, and perhaps even in the collection of Mary Gaunt's Granny. These things started their journey as plunder and trophy, but large and small, whether ivory cricket palaces, magic fountains or whole gardens, curios and their procurement can be subject to tricks of perspective. Perfect clarity is not an option.

The looting of the Yuan Ming Yuan was not entirely the work of foreigners, as Hope Danby and, more recently Geremie Barmé, have pointed out, and it is still being looted, turned into playing cards and stamps, stripped of its last remaining real treasure, its shared melancholy, as it is converted into a symbol of resurgent national pride – and potential future conflict.

15. A Window in the Forest

The photo on facing page shows a glass window, from the ruins of a mid-nineteenth-century church in a forest in south-western China, built just a little before the destruction of the *Yuan Ming Yuan*. Apart from its context as part of a Christian church window, this *use* of glass might be considered, from the Chinese point of view, a curio of Western culture since, in a Chinese tradition that persisted into the late seventeenth century, when it began to be made in factories and used in the Forbidden City, glass was principally a material for decorative or ritual purposes rather than a building material. It was used for tomb ornaments, grave offerings and various vessels hundreds of years before it even appeared with the Mediterranean trade of the Silk Roads, and was in use perhaps as far back as the time of Confucius (6th Century BCE). According to ancient Chinese Taoist and later Gandharan Indian Buddhist cosmology, both jade and glass have cosmological significance, and objects made from these shiny, other-worldly materials were fashioned into distinctively Chinese objects such as dragons and cicadas. In fact *liu li,* an old term for shiny surfaces is still visible today in Beijing, in the name of a famous street of Chinese antiques, bookshops and curios that was once the site of the factory that made glazed tiles for the Forbidden City and Imperial Palace complex. You can go there still – to *Liu Li Chang Jie,* (琉璃长街 'The Street of the Factory of Glazed Tiles'), a twenty-minute walk from Matteo Ricci's Southern Cathedral – and buy a variety of things from genuine antiques to shiny masterpieces of kitsch. For visitors it has long been known as the street for souvenirs and at least until the '90s it was possible to go beneath the shops into cellars, where you could find some very interesting pieces.

This particular piece of glass is part of a church window on the rural outskirts of Guiyang city in Guizhou Province, south-western China. The *Lu Chong Guan* Catholic Church and Monastery, reclaimed by nature to the extent that local information describes the ruins as 'buried in the depths of Guizhou Province's botanical district', contains a monastery (St Paul's, built by a French missionary between 1854 and 1856), and a church of the Assumption of the Virgin Mary, built in 1873. The original monastery was closed in 1956, becoming the site of Guizhou Psychiatric Hospital, (what passes among aliens for evidence of divinity may well seem a form of collective madness among locals) then finally part of Guizhou Botanical Gardens in the 1980s. The Church of the Assumption was badly damaged in the Cultural Revolution, and all that remains is a brick wall about ten metres high, the lower stone foundations and three remaining windows. The site of the original monastery was discovered during a survey of cultural relics in 2015 and in 2018 it was placed under the protection of the Guizhou Cultural Relics

Unit. I hope it fares better than Xun Huisheng's old home in Beijing.

The remaining three windows have Western-style stained glass but the panes are contained in a vermilion and cobalt lattice reminiscent of Chinese design, now obscured by vines and creepers. It's a rather fitting symbol of intercultural perspective. If you observe the window from the outside, that is from the outside of a trespassing edifice of foreign-ness, you may see a temple of perverted Western idolatry, an alien monument transplanted from another world, now being reclaimed by its original and rightful Chinese environment. If you look from the inside of an edifice of belief you may see the native environment not as an agent of reclamation but as a force of regression, the reinstatement of wild and ungoverned wilderness, of profligate, unredeemed nature encroaching upon a sanctuary of hard-won civilisation and enlightenment. And if you stand at some distance from the church, allowing it to fade to a blurred impression like that 3-D puzzle, imagining another time and place, gazing not into the church but into the ruins of an idea, you may be able to appreciate both the passionate dream that put the temple there in that unlikely place – and something of the fear that greeted its arrival from another world.

However, between the foundation of the original monastery and the building of the second church, Christianity took an indigenous form in China. The Taiping Rebellion (or Civil War, as some historians prefer to call it), raged throughout southern and central China from 1850 to 1864, crippling the Qing Dynasty and leaving an estimated 20-30 million dead in its wake, with an equal number of displaced persons; one of humanity's most catastrophic descents into warfare – and all without the aid of twentieth century weapons of mass destruction. Hong Xiuquan, a Hakka man (*Kejia*, 客家, a southern Chinese minority), influenced by Christian missionaries, and believing himself to be the younger brother of Jesus Christ, led a catastrophic armed revolution, establishing a capital in Nanjing from which to establish his Utopian syncretic-Christian 'Great Peace Heavenly Kingdom' in place of a weak and corrupt Confucian dynasty. I don't wish to be flippant, in view of the appalling bloodshed and suffering, but you could be excused for thinking of a certain contemporary American political evangelist.

China had seen many occasions for the violent transfer of power from one dynasty to another, but the Taiping Rebellion was in essence a revolutionary social movement, involving, among other things, re-distribution of land, prohibition of opium importation, the abolition of foot-binding and radical forms of social equality believed by many historians to be the antecedent of later revolution. But, from the Taiping Rebellion to the Boxer Uprising, and the last days of the Qing dynasty, China's quest for social reform and self-realisation was enveloped in a fog of misunderstanding. It was, like the window in the forest, a small opening, inevitably strangled by encroaching vines of ignorance and fear.

The period of this church-in-the-jungle, from the mid-nineteenth century to the end of the First World War, including the May Fourth Movement, a protest at the betrayal of China after the Treaty of Versailles, was a struggle for the regeneration of a nation that was crumbling from within while it succumbed to violation from without, a nation stranded between the Gates of Dynastic

Sleep and the Gates of Revolutionary Dreams. For many foreigners however, China itself became a vast curio, another ivory cage suspended above realities, through which passed the oft-deluded dreams and supporting myths of martial and mercantile conquerors, adventurers in pursuit of exotic treasures and devout missionaries bent on conversion of the Chinese to an alien god. The revolutionary dream, on the other hand, was yet to take coherent narrative form but it was presaged by the self-sustaining and self-destructive myth of the Boxers, the 'Society of Righteous and Harmonious Fists' (*Yi He Quan*). This is the name which led to the translation 'Boxers', indicating a Chinese martial arts component, but some argue the name should be translated as something like 'volunteer-together society', the fist connoting tight-clenched unity rather than 'boxing'. In any case there was certainly violence involved. The illustration below, showing the three-character name, is from the cover of *China and the Allies*, (1901) by Alfred Henry Savage-Landor.

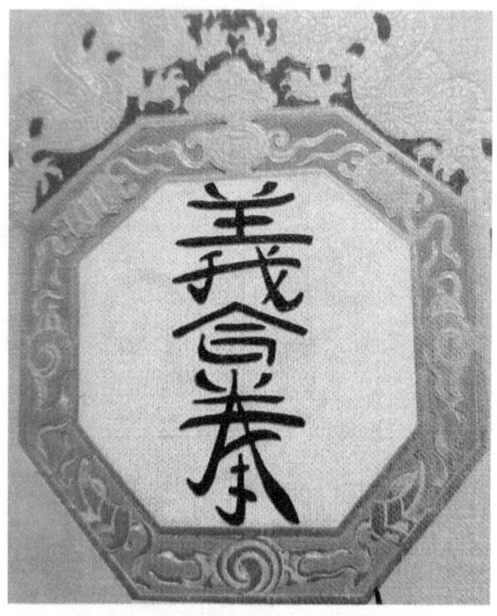

Savage-Landor (1865-1924), grandson of the poet Walter Savage Landor, was an English painter, writer, traveller and WWI designer of tanks and airships, who provided a (literally) graphic, boy's own (although rather more like AO) account of his exploits and travails in Tibet in a very popular and sensational book, *In the Forbidden Land*, (1898), in which he describes his capture and torture by feral Tibetans. He travelled in China during the Boxer Uprising and wrote a two-volume account of the conflict, including descriptions of the life and customs of the Chinese.

The picture on the facing page is also from Savage-Landor's book, his drawing of a 'Boxer'. The word-picture below is by Fred Whiting (1873-1962), British illustrator at *The Graphic* and *The Daily Graphic*, who provided coverage of the Uprising for its duration throughout 1900 and 1901:

A party of about thirty Boxers, apparently headed off, were facing the Germans, and going through their dance, or Boxer movements. They were led by a man on a white horse. He wore, like most of these people, bright red sashes and shoulder belts, and a bright coloured cloth wound round his head. The Boxers were armed with Manlicher rifles, spears and swords but the whole of them were shot down in a short time, while four of our men were wounded. Each Boxer carries in a sort of pouch made of cloth – worn like a sporran – a charm, a piece of paper on which are written in blood Chinese characters, which the poor fellow thinks will render him impervious to the bullets of the foreigner. He also holds the belief that if a man is killed by foreign soldiers he will come to life again in seven days.

In view of Christian beliefs about resurrection you can't help feeling their misplaced faith in a life after foreign bullets is not entirely the fault of native superstition. And as I read the next paragraph I am even more conscious of the 'ethnic image and superscription' inherent in religious beliefs. One person's temple is another's joss-house; one person's god is another's idol.

After the fight we camped for the night in the village, the general and staff selecting the Temple to sleep in. Being pitch dark, and cold, we were glad, after some trouble in getting wood, to cook our supper and turn in. Seeing a blaze, I went to find out what it was, and saw the soldiers throwing the idols of the joss-house into a big fire, to make room for their quarters for the night.

The movement, 1899-1901, was anti-foreign and anti-Christian, and for a time supported the Qing government, until it failed and its members found themselves exposing their necks to the blunt swords of cattle butchers who, despite being fuelled with alcohol, took five or six swings to behead their victims, the corpses left exposed for spectators until noon. The uprising (it was not really a 'rebellion', although it is often so-styled), culminated in the most well-known incident of the period, in which foreign diplomats, missionaries, troops – and some Chinese Christians – retreated to the Legation Quarter, inside the southeastern walls of the Tartar City, where they were, for '55 Days at Beijing', besieged by the Boxers until relieved by a 20,000-strong eight-nation alliance that did not include Charlton Heston. The drawing below indicates somethng of the arrogance and effrontery – followed by looting and slaughter – that accompanied the relief of the Legation.

12. East and West: A Group of Officers at the Gate of the Forbidden City, Peking
Artist: Gordon Browne, from a sketch by a correspondent
Published: 8 December 1900 in *The Graphic*
Size: 13" x 17 1/2"
Medium: Gouache on board

A bunch of British, Japanese, Russian, German, American, French and Italian officers (and a stray dog, exemplifying the adage 'a cat may look at a king'), are shown lounging around an impotent lion-dog guardian at the entrance to the Forbidden City. It was accompanied by this text:

> Whatever the jealousies felt in Diplomatic quarters and fostered by the Press of rival Powers, the officers of the International troops are on the best of terms, fraternizing most amicably.

But the gestures depicted seem to indicate an international fraternity based on mockery of the vanquished.

There's scant evidence of respect for China's 'great organic conceptions' in the attitudes of soldiers of the great powers assembled around the lion-dog in this drawing, but neither was there respect among Chinese officials for the 'various barbarians' who had presumed to trespass upon the dragon throne with their preposterous claims to equality, their quaint vassal-state myth of history and destiny. The word 'myth' is now so debased I hesitate to use it, but as Joseph Campbell (*The Hero with a Thousand Faces*) says of mythic heroes, they bring the means of regeneration to their people. China's myth of regeneration is an epic tale of 'one hundred years of humiliation' that began with the Opium Wars in the mid-nineteenth century and is supposed to end with the reclamation of Taiwan, a story endlessly repeated throughout China today, a 'meme' in contemporary terms, a story not just of regeneration but of dragons chasing their tales in a cycle of destiny. The myth of the dragon throne and the aloof, self-sufficient, inviolable majesty of Chinese imperial culture ended, or paused, with the Opium Wars, the Boxer Uprising, the Old Buddha Ci Xi and the 'last emperor' Pu Yi, but a new and frighteningly powerful dragon-myth has taken its place.

16. Picnic at the Sleeping Dragon Pine: Idylls of Old Peking

'The last days of old Peking' was a drama played out by foreign soldiers, missionaries, merchants and even hermits, but as John K. Fairbank reminds us, Beijing itself had been 'a capital city of non-Chinese conquerors and Chinese collaborators for most of a thousand years'.

Foreign residents enjoyed Peking all the more after 1900, when allied Christendom (plus Japan) suppressed the Boxer effort to expel them. From 1901 to 1937 (at which point new conquerors came) was a rare and happy time for foreigners in Peking, an era of special perquisites and a special freedom of opportunity, not least to participate in the fringe of Chinese life without being stuck in it. Like Mongol chieftains of the thirteenth century, when Polo saw Cambaluc, or Manchu captains of the seventeenth, when Father Schall headed the astronomical bureau, foreigners in Peking in the early 1900s had an untouchable status (newly

known as extra-territoriality) and lived in their own cultural fashion, variously racing their ponies or worshipping their god.

This was the idyllic time for foreigners depicted in a very popular novel of the time, *Peking Picnic*, 1932, by Anne Bridge (Mary Dolling Sanders, 1889-1974, wife of a Foreign Office official). Picnics in the Western Hills were *de rigueur*. The photo above (author photo, 2017), shows 'The Sleeping Dragon Pine', a centuries-old pine in the Ordination Terrace Temple (*Jie Tai Si*, 戒台寺). The temple, and the pine, are of uncertain age, but there are, or were, steles of great antiquity in the temple grounds, including one from the Liao Dynasty (916-1125 CE), as well as numerous very ancient white pines and ginkgos. This is one of eight temples favoured by nineteenth and twentieth century foreigners, with family and friends – and ponies – for picnics. There's another famous book of the time called *Peonies and Ponies*, by Sir Harold Acton, a British writer of Anglo-Italian heritage, who lived in Beijing (1932-39), and studied Chinese drama and poetry. He used to say, when it came to the lives of foreigners in Beijing, fact was stranger than fiction, but strangely, made no mention of the murder of Pamela Werner in his writing.

Anyway, this is Anne Bridge's lovely description of the temple:

Chie T'ai Ssu [*Jie Tai Si*], The Monastery of the Platform of Vows, stands on a sort of natural terrace just below the crest of one of the ridges running down from the Western Hills towards the Peking plain, flanking the valley of the Hun-ho on the south. Its innumerable courts, pavilions, shrines and terraces stretch up the hill-side, one above another, connected by paved walks and broad flights of marble steps, scattered irregularly in all directions at all sorts of levels; diversified by trees springing from the stone pavements, by rocky landscapes and grottoes in corners, by little pagodas, by Drum Towers and Bell Towers, and by vast bronze incense-burners – the whole beautiful confusion, covering several acres and containing as many souls as an English village, enclosed within a high wall which follows its irregular outline over the contours of the steep stony slopes. Men in bright flower-blue cassocks, with blue trousers tucked in white gaiter boots, wander about its shade-splashed walks and disappear through its unexpected doorways; grey-robed priests tend its latticed shrines, filling the courts with the perfume of incense, beat its vast resonant drums and its musical gongs; or stand in dreamy meditation, rosary in hand, beside its carved marble balustrades.

But this was also the time of many whose excursions and incursions far exceeded ponies and picnics, the time of George Morrison, Reginald Johnston, James Stewart Lockhart and of course Edmund Backhouse, who, Fairbank notes, surpassed all of these in not just engaging with Chinese but in 'going native'.

On the facing page is another of my special curios, an inscription, in a 1921 book on Chinese drama written by Reginald Johnston, tutor to Aisin Gioro, Pu Yi, 'The Last Emperor'; a dedication to his mentor Sir James Lockhart Stewart, a former Colonial Commissioner of Wei Hai Wei in north-east China. (To add to its provenance the book was formerly owned by John Minford, distinguished and prolific translator of many Chinese classics.)

Johnstone, from 1927-30, was the last such commissioner of Wei Hai Wei, (which included a walled city, part of a whole territory on the Shandong Peninsula, not just a port), leased to Britain 1898-1930, one of the concessions extracted from China during 'the century of humiliations'. Wei Hai Wei, under the British, had hospitals, churches, sports grounds, post offices and a cemetery

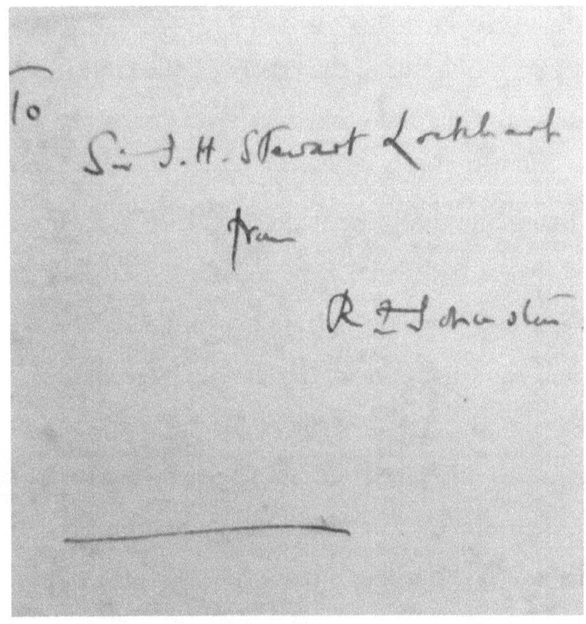

– and a hybrid flag consisting of a Union Jack and an imperial dragon, symbol of the Qing dynasty. Lockhart had the dragon replaced by mandarin ducks enclosed in a leafy ring, but at least he kept a Chinese presence – and a symbol of harmony – although the territory, like others, was subject to extra-territoriality, in which British subjects were not subject to Chinese law. The incursions, territorial and cultural, that started with the Treaty of Nanjing (1842), and the ceding of Hong Kong to Britain were a source of affront, a violation of China's idea of itself, allowing for free British trade with China and even a penalty in which China was forced to pay damages for destroyed opium.

Perhaps the most entrancing tale of all from the 'last days of Old Peking' concerns the fate of fourteen ancient bronze incense-burners that once 'lived' in the Eastern Study of the ancestral home of David Kidd's wife Aimee. These, largest of which was about the size of a saucepan, sat in the centre of one table, flanked by six smaller burners, while the other seven were arranged on a second table:

> The unique thing about these incense burners was that they always had to be kept burning. They had been in Aimee's charge from the time her father had become bed-ridden, and he had given her detailed instruction in their history and care. Unlike the ancient, intricately patterned, and patina-encrusted Chinese bronze sacrificial vessels that are in the world's museums, these bronzes were clean and smooth and comparatively new, having been cast only five hundred years ago. However, according to Aimee, their like had never been made before or since.

The burners were made from a mixture of the melted gold left after a fire in the palace of a Ming emperor, a shipment of fine red copper from Burma and some ground rubies from Turkestan, combined 'by the alchemist's art' and mixed with other substances to create bronze objects 'of unexcelled beauty', created for ritual use. A brick of burning charcoal was placed in the middle of each and smothered with the ash of previously burnt incense, on top of which was placed a new stick of sandalwood incense. The charcoal kept the bronze hot and applied slow heat to the stick, which then began to emit its distinctive aroma. These fourteen burners had never been allowed to cool in five hundred years, their charcoal cores replaced every two or three days:

They were magical objects, glowing and shimmering like jewels, no two alike. Some were red; others were speckled with iridescent green or with twinkling bits of ruby or gold. When Aimee had explained their origin to me, she went to a cabinet and brought out an incense burner of exquisite shape but of a dull, brassy color. "This is what would happen if the fire went out," she said.

'Couldn't you build another fire in it?' I asked.

'Of course," Aimee said, 'but nothing would happen. Once the burner is allowed to go entirely cold, the color fades and no later heat can bring it back.'

But Aimee had a premonition that something dreadful was going to happen, and her worst fears were soon realised. Kidd found her early one morning gazing in horror at one of the incense burners:

She quickly put it down and picked up another. Then she touched all the rest of them. 'They're all cold!' she wailed, and collapsed into a chair.

They looked cold. All the color and life was gone, leaving them the color of a brass doorknob. I picked one burner up. The ash in the center was slightly damp; water had been poured into it. We found that each pot had been watered just enough to put out its fire.

A servant girl, her resentments fuelled by revolutionary lessons at school, about parasitic remnants of the feudal past such as those her family had served for generations, had put out the five-hundred-year-old flames. Simple. But what of Aimee's premonition? Of course she *would* have premonitions, all part of her traditional culture, and anyway, with the world changing around her, why wouldn't she have the feeling that something bad was going to happen – if not today, maybe tomorrow? But these prosaic realities are easily reconciled with Aimee's psychic intuitions. The servant girl may be seen in two quite different ways: as the instrument of modern revolutionary rationalism, burning in her own way with generations of righteous indignation, or even plain old jealousy, finally dousing the self-serving myth of a privileged Confucian scholar-gentry family; or as the instrument of a prophecy of some kind, connecting the fate of the family – and Beijing itself – with the life of the incense-burners in a manner beloved of world myths and folktales. It makes little difference which interpretation you choose, and either will do as a respectful way of looking at the 'last days of Old Peking'.

17. The Bamboo Poem

There's a scroll in my study, a rubbing from an early six-teenth-century stone in The Forest of Steles in Xi'an. It's so long I can't even hang it on a wall, I had to lay it out on the dining room table just to photograph it, and even then I could only manage it in sections. I've had it for years but never troubled to study it because it's so unwieldy. As I unrolled it for the photo on the preceding page, I became engrossed in a historical record, an anthology, a riddle, a record of provenance and an illustrated manuscript.

At the top are four characters in the seal script of the Qin Dynasty (221-206 BCE), *Guan Di Shi Zhu*, 'A Bamboo Poem for Emperor Guan'. Underneath are two stems of bamboo. In the top right- hand corner, in the section shown above, there's an enigmatic object that had me mystified for some time. It looks like a cashbox, four rings attached to the handle of a steel box. It reminded me of Jacob Marley's chains in *A Christmas Carol* – perhaps it was a manacle or yoke of some kind used in a Chinese punishment for usury. Recently I peered into the bamboo more carefully. I felt it wanted to tell me something – and so it did. I thought I could detect the outline of Chinese characters formed by the leaves of the bamboo, but I wasn't sure. I took the scroll to a learned Chinese friend, but for a time she wasn't convinced they were characters at all. They just didn't look right. Then she began to pick them out, one by one, until they emerged as a poem. I was rather proud of myself and made a bit of a song and dance about it, but I think the advantage I had over her was that I'm used to seeing Chinese characters that just don't look right – that is, the way I write them.

We looked up details of the scroll by means of her on-line Chinese encyclopedia, The 'emperor' is Guan Yu, a general of the Three Kingdoms Period (220-280 CE), given the honorary status of emperor, although he was in fact a provincial governor. He is a household name among educated Chinese even today as a result of traditional hagiography and the fourteenth-century Chinese historical novel *Romance of the Three Kingdoms*. But back to the cashbox…the detail spreading out from the clump of bamboo forms a kind of story-rhizome. It's a seal 'book', used for containing a seal or stamp, the signature – like 'ex libris' – of the original commissioner of the engraving. And there below the mysterious object, out of range of the picture above, is the stamp, inscribed *Han Shou Ting Yin* – the official seal of the lord or 'marquis' of Han Shou village.

If I'm going to be fascinated by anything it's a rubbing; shadows and silhouettes coaxed from stone in an ancient ritual of invocation. A special kind of moistened paper is inserted into the engraving, carefully tapped down with a wooden mallet, poked deep into the incisions with a brush and, when dry, brushed again with a pad of inked silk until the images emerge in intaglio from black borders of raised sections and white recesses of untouched paper. This elaborate procedure has produced an impression of the bamboo canes carved into the stone, and the lines of verse on each side of the two canes – one upright, the other bending. The seal book and stamp appear at the top. The stamp is that of an official of the Ming Dynasty in the eighteenth year of the Ming Emperor Hongzhi (1505 CE, the year of the emperor's death at the age of 34). Hongzhi was noted for the probity of his reign, running an upright Confucian form of government in which corrupt officials were dismissed from office. He is also noted for his un-emperor like behaviour in that he is reputed to be one of only two Chinese emperors who did not help himself to concubines.

The characters disguised in the leaves of the bamboo constitute a four-line, five-character-per-line classical Chinese poem (a particular metre and rhyme system – *wu yan jue ju shi*, 五言绝句诗), commemorating 'Emperor' Guan, suggesting that a righteous official is like the fresh green bamboo outcrop with its supple canes and slender leaves; upright when required and capable of bending without breaking when required, independent and strong, symbolising steadfast loyalty and righteousness of the sometimes solitary and austere kind.

So far so good, but I was only part-way there. There is a multimedia, multi-textual story embedded here in this rubbing, a dialogue across millennia between poetry and history, and even a kind of intercultural numeracy involved in working out dates, since they are recorded in terms of imperial reign periods. The rubbing contains another carved seal-stamp, this one from the fifty-fifth year of the Kang Xi Emperor – 1716 CE. Seal-stamping was a habit of scholar-gentry officials (and emperors) over the dynastic period, so you can detect distinct layers of history in the colophons of successive owners. The official seal-stamp title conferred upon the original owner, the Marquis, indicates that he is a worthy successor to 'Emperor Guan' of the third century CE, and I presume, by implication, to the Emperor Hongzhi himself. The rubbing, mounted on silk and fixed in porcelain rollers, is thus a composite tribute to three righteous officials spanning fifteen hundred years. As its most recent owner I have refrained from adding to its provenance. I don't say I could be considered a model of upright behaviour but at least I have restricted myself to collecting curios rather than concubines. I don't get enough credit for that.

As for the bamboo poem, I love its form, something that might have inspired e.e.cummings or Ezra Pound…or Bob Winter. People often say, misleadingly, that the Chinese script is pictographic, and so it was, at some point before the seal script shown above evolved from Bronze Age ritual engravings, but no script can sustain the full complexities of language in a series of stylised pictures. It will straight away run into the hurdle of abstract ideas – like loyalty and righteousness. But this poem is something else. It is built on symbols, characters representing words representing meanings, words with dual meanings, as in metaphor, but it also mimics the *source* of the metaphor itself – the leaves of the bamboo. It's a pictographic poem. I'm reminded again of e.e.cummings and that poem intended to mimic the movement of a grasshopper. I'm thinking too of the streetside water-calligraphers I've seen in south-west China, who dip a mop into a bucket and brush water-characters onto a pavement. Exquisitely-formed characters from an epigram, poem or novel appear briefly and then vanish, suggesting the Taoist-Buddhist idea of impermanence. The movement of the brush, of the calligrapher-performer and the water itself are integrated in an enactment of the ephemeral. My rubbing is derived from the solid reality of stone – but still it has this quality of something not-real, an illusion. Shadows on stone.

It's not a point about impermanence I want to make, however. It's to do with the way all things, inscribed in all sorts of ways, may be read in all kinds of scripts; sometimes by geologists in the way of rivers of ice carving their way through mountains, sometimes by psychoanalysts in the way of dreams and memories, sometimes by linguists and archaeologists in the way of scratches on shards of pottery, sometimes by historians in the way of recorded names and dates, sometimes by fossil-hunters in the way of dragons in rocks – and sometimes by collectors in the way of curios.

18. Curios, Fetishes and the Madness of Crowds

The great English fossil-hunter and pioneer of palaeontology, Mary Anning, hapless victim of a deplorable recent movie in which she is played, and fore-played, as a repressed but fast-learning lesbian, sold 'snake stones' and 'devil's fingers' in her parents' curio shop in Lyme Regis – fossilised ammonites, ichthyosaurs and plesiosaurs, marine reptiles that had been poking up out of the rubble of eroded coastal limestone and shale for countless generations of people to find and think of in all kinds of imaginative and folkloric ways until they became decipherable as a script engraved in stone by life itself. Uninformed speculation and wrong guesses about the meaning of that script were never so great a barrier to understanding as the lack of curiosity engendered by the biblical certainties of *Genesis*. In the world of Mary Anning's religious contemporaries, the Devil, the 'Old Serpent', was believed to have strewn a false trail of serpent-like clues throughout the cliffs of Lyme Regis in order to deceive and distract the faithful. Right-thinking, pious people knew that God had fashioned all the creatures of the earth, all the fishes of the deep and all the fowls of the air exactly as they were in their day, in a single act of creation that took place six thousand years ago. Such people did not want to know any different, and ironically, it took a collector of the Devil's decoy dragons to provide a means of seeing a real one. For a great many people that faith-threatening reality could not have been more frightening.

A novel about Mary Anning was published in 2010 with the title of *Curiosity: A Love Story*, by Joan Thomas. It's a remarkable book, but I'm beginning to think poor Mary has been attracting belated attention for all the wrong reasons, just as her discoveries attracted attention for all the wrong reasons, as sea-side novelties. In view of what I've been saying I suppose I can hardly now claim there are right and wrong reasons for being curious about her or her discoveries. Still, I can't help wondering why her extraordinary intellectual life, her largely unassisted and long-unacknowledged triumph of reason over the dogma of her betters, isn't enough to sustain fascination, why it is necessary to dwell on the ordinary physical and emotional needs she had in common with most of humanity. 'We do not know what the dragon *means*, just as we do not know the meaning of the universe', say Jose Luis Borges and Margarita Guerrero in *The Book of Imaginary Beings*. 'Dragons' of the Jurassic are at least a clue to the meaning of the universe in the Mary Anning story, and much of the abiding contemporary significance of her story lies in the way so many people were sorely afraid of the real thing, of its lesson, engraved in the cliffs, that nothing is permanent, that untold numbers of species come and go by the whim of nature, that the history of life on earth is not to be read in a venerated human text received via ascribed supernatural authority, but in the rocks and minerals inscribed by nature, in the 'snakestones' of Lyme Regis. To echo Borges and Guerrero once more, Mary's dragons were a 'necessary monster'.

Both Werner and Winter have portrayed the scariest 'real' dragon of them all — not some supreme creator, benign or malign, but the accidental universe that creates and destroys whole worlds of species, and even, ultimately, stones. Winter denounces humanity's fear of scientific knowledge and refusal to accept the reality of a godless world. Werner quotes Schiller 'Who can enjoy life if he sees into its depths?' Those depths frighten me too as I gaze into my curios. I can't now look at photos of the great mass rallies of Mao's adoring revolutionary youth in Tian An Men Square in August 1966 without being reminded that the blind worm of dogmatism and fanaticism has been securely lodged in the human brain in all cultures throughout history and is continuing to glut itself on the rare delicacies of reason and tolerance. That such things come and go with fashion, the result of 'extraordinary popular delusions and the madness of crowds' as Charles Mackay put it in 1841, is evident in recent history, in which China went through a brief period of self-reflection manifested in the arts and political philosophy, only to return to even stricter orthodoxy.

The two photos below were taken during visits I made to the avant-garde galleries that sprang up in arts precincts on the outskirts of Beijing between the late 1980s and early 2000s, often featuring what might be termed Mao-morabilia, a very special, often edgy, ironically nostalgic, genre of curios.

This slogan, on the wall of a hangar-like building that could be a disused factory or an air-raid shelter, reads 'Ten Thousand Years to Chairman Mao', in very faded and flaking red paint, and is left to make its own simple and very obvious, almost innocent, point. The photo on facing page shows art of the much more contrived kind, involving a different shade of red; in fact its lustre is in stark contrast to the faded rubric invoking longevity for Mao. Two highly lacquered tutelary goddesses of the *Red Detachment of Women* (one of the revolutionary modern ballets of the Cultural Revolution), guard a sacred relic of the 'Mao suit' kind – in fact a tunic originally associated with Sun Yat-sen, former president of the republic. The garment, apart from its emptiness, has a deeper meaning for older Chinese people, recalling the symbolic numerology of an earlier Chinese revolution – its four pockets, five large central buttons and three small sleeve buttons representing the four virtues, five powers and three principles that were to represent New China. The powers of executive and judiciary were supposed to be separated on this garment of state.

The warriors of the Red Detachment of Women Modern Revolutionary Ballet Troupe are modestly kitted-out in snugly-fitting and very long shorts, designed to frustrate any audience participation of the up-skirting kind, but which nevertheless drove young men of the era wild with revolutionary passion and class feeling. Buttocks and breasts are thrust into prominence by high-heeled shoes while the shapely red limbs arising from them are unfettered by their thin veneer of glossy cladding. They are watched at a distance by a miniature figure, perhaps a young Mao, in an incongruously dowdy and ill-fitting proletarian prototype of the later tailored tunics and caps that tourists could once not get enough of. Between the sentinel sirens, for reasons I am still pondering, are two cross-sections of a tree, its still-green growth rings split by some catastrophic event, a red asteroid perhaps. I don't have detail of the artist, but for reasons that will become apparent, it reminds me of the work of Guo Jian, who has exhibited in Australia and internationally since the 1990s. In an interview with Linda Jaivin, he once said of *Red Detachment of Women*:

> I loved it. We all did. Why? Thinking back, it's got to be all those women in shorts! At the time, you never got to see women's legs. But you could go to *The Red Detachment of Women* without anyone calling you a hooligan or suspecting your motives. In China, sexuality carries a negative connotation. You don't admit to sexual desire. But even army propaganda used subtle sexual imagery to draw us in.

It also reminds me of one of those kitsch souvenir barometers, with the tree-rings, and the 'hands' formed by the split sections, representing some kind of chronometer, perhaps suggesting times of madness, then and now. In the same interview Guo Jian refers to the Cultural Revolution as a 'mind-fucking drug'. If so, it was a designer drug.

These works of art and archness, sometimes styled 'cynical realism', itself a cynical parody of a major element of Cultural Revolution aesthetic theory, make me think again about forms of madness, about 'the Great Proletarian Cultural Revolution', to give it its proper name. What was 'cultural' about it? Was it something as banal as fashion, no more than a pernicious form of political costume drama, exploiting the need of people to belong, to be included, to signal their legitimate status as insiders by means of their fervent and conspicuous rejection of outsiders?

Charles Mackay articulates the underlying issue as well as anyone, today, or in his own time, 183 years ago:

> In reading the history of nations, we find that, like individuals, they have their whims and their peculiarities, their seasons of excitement and recklessness, when they care not what they do. We find that whole communities suddenly fix their minds upon one object, and go mad in its pursuit; that millions of people become similarly impressed with one delusion, and run after it, till their attention is caught by some new folly more captivating than the first.

Other than my own theatre items, including my collection of various iterations of the 'model operas', I can't bring myself to collect relics of the Cultural Revolution. I caught a glimpse of the madness of crowds during my visits to China in the '70s and I still fear it greatly. I can't even look at pictures of the lovely numinous Xi'er, 'The White-Haired Girl', in full revolutionary-balletic flight, without being reminded of the way we are again today fashioning 'revolutionary modern dramas' out of complex past events and reducing cultural diversity to some kind of identity parade. In some ways the whole premise of this book, that it is possible to find one's way into an 'inner city' of understanding through outer gates of intelligent, albeit uninformed, curiosity, is under threat from those who regard this not only as an intrusion into *their* forbidden city but a form of cultural theft or 'appropriation'. Trespassers beware. These truculent gatekeepers seem to think we must all know our place and remain confined within some kind of cis-cultural legation quarter. I've been lucky in my chosen field of interest in that I have never encountered this attitude in any of the Chinese friends and colleagues I have come to know. In all these fifty years, I have yet to meet a Chinese person who thinks that, as a foreigner, I should not write books about China, although I have to admit I have met one or two who thought I *could* not. To put it another way, if you tell Chinese acquaintances you are studying *qi gong* or *tai ji* they will express approval, even admiration. At worst they may not take you seriously, and there may even be a bit of condescension, but they certainly won't be offended or threatened.

But…the picture on the facing page, taken from a 1957 folio of Beijing opera costumes, suggests even some dragons can take fright at human ideological fashions. Perhaps he'd got wind of Mao's 1942 speech at the Yan'an Forum on Literature and the Arts, bad news not only for dragons and phoenixes, but for emperors, generals, scholars, ghosts, concubines, judges and lords, the stuff of traditional mythology, theatre, literature – and curios.

19. The Meaning of the Dragon

The bamboo poem in Chapter 17 shows us that what you take from a curio depends on how you learn to read its 'script'. Dragons are among the most enticing of Chinese curios, since, along with phoenixes, tigers and tortoises, their mysterious power has been represented in bone, bronze and jade since the Shang Dynasty (16th-11th centuries BCE). You can discern the dragon's serpentine contours in the oracle bone script of the Shang, in the bronze and seal scripts of the first millennium BCE, in the traditional written form, and even in the simplified form used today in the Peoples Republic of China. The nearer you approach the present the harder your imagination has to work, but the dragon survives.

I really like the first of these shown below, in seal script, a third century BCE ancestor of the others. I can't look at it without thinking of a pair of dragons doing the highland fling, and the night when, fuelled with the famous 'Moutai' local sorghum liquor, I demonstrated a highly-improvised form of highland dancing for a group of Miao minority women in Guiyang. I invited my ostensibly spellbound audience to participate only to find they were all better at it than me. That's me on the left-hand side of the first character, wearing my Hay tartan Tam o' Shanter and a Miao souvenir table-runner for a kilt.

龍 龙

Dragons are never far from the Gates of Dreams, luring us beyond with fascination and fear. As I look at the first of the characters shown above, its shape derived from the Shang form used in the ritual of divination and sacrifice, in which blood-anointed incisions in ox clavicles and turtle plastrons were burned with heated rods to produce cracks that could be read as prophecies, I experience awe – I suppose that *is* a kind of fear after all. But what of Lord Ye Gong? What are we to make of this man whose fixation has become little more than a veiled and vague admonition? What is the meaning of the dragon? Was Lord Ye the man who loved to collect but couldn't commit, as in love and relationships? That's not so far removed from John Blofeld, frightened by his own shallowness in immersing himself in the self-destruction of passion rather than the self-denial of love:

Lying awake by her side, I found myself appalled. However powerfully I resisted it, the knowledge that my love had already begun to spiral down towards its own extinction was now rooted in my mind. Though I could not foresee the speed with which this would happen, I was already faced with a dim realisation that ignorance, inexperience and childish romanticism had combined to lure me into passing off a long-suppressed yearning of the loins as a true yearning of the heart, thus mistaking swiftly withering autumn leaves for the purest gold! Perhaps the sham of that deception would be with me yet, if I had not one day come to know that a true yearning of the heart is something no mortal woman can ever wholly satisfy!

This paragraph takes me down a path I truly fear – the path that leads me from Blofeld's notion of Mind, a state of absorption into some great ineffable Buddhist One-ness, to Werner and his inexorable, pitiless Space-Time Universe. So back to dragons, to the safer grounds of worldly parable. Are we meant to think Ye Gong got a terrible fright because, for all his fascination with dragons, he didn't really *believe* in them? There are people who can't get enough of ghost *stories* and yet scoff at those superstitious folk who actually believe in ghosts. As I said in the beginning, I was a bit like that myself once but then I got to know some very well-educated Chinese who believe, who employ shamans with their mysterious talisman-scripts and cinnabar powder rings to protect them from ghosts and demons. This surprised me at first, but when I think about it, and listen carefully to the stories I've been told, such people are reacting to ghosts and malignant spirits in the same way they might react to any other dangerous phenomenon that is part of the 'natural' universe, just as they might react to the sudden appearance of a crocodile in their swimming pool – unexpected, inexplicable, terrifying – but entirely 'natural'. I, on the other hand, would be robbed of my senses by the appearance of a ghost because I don't *believe* in them. The manifestation of such beings would not only threaten *me* but my whole view of nature. To paraphrase Ai Weiwei, 'It is important to think about what you really don't believe in. It could kill you.' Then there is the question of what is real and what is not, as if they cannot co-exist somewhere beyond our cage of senses – and I think too of that other arbitrary distinction between fiction and non-fiction. How are we to interpret the mystery and dread of Varè's story about a Mongolian shaman and his ability to make people live their lives immured in bewitching, sometimes horrifying, dreams? Is there truth in the illusion?

The tormented E T.C. Werner was lured beyond the Gates of Dreams. He conjured up a multitude of wonderful, fantastic dragons in his research into Chinese folklore but kept superstition at arm's length with deeply rational, scientific and philosophical thought about the nature of the universe. What he saw at last however, was the real dragon of a universe 'without a heart', in the form of his own unwittingly Delphic prophecy and the remains of poor, eviscerated Pamela, tossed semi-naked onto a heap of rubbish at the foot of the 'Fox Tower' just ten years after he wrote the fateful words I quoted earlier in this book. When I first read about this I thought of Werner as a character in one of M.R. James's 'ghost stories of an antiquary', whistling up some dread, mocking curse of the cosmos with all his detached and scholarly poking about among Chinese ghosts and goblins, things that may have been better left undisturbed, unexplained – and un-believed-in. I see it differently now. He always understood the nature of the real dragon, as opposed to the collectables, but nevertheless, when it appeared it was beyond his imagining.

Perhaps I'm making too much of a homely old proverb that could mean anything. Perhaps it's simply a lesson to me – I've spent my life loving the dragon and now I have come to fear it. But that's assuming I have at last encountered the 'real' dragon. Perhaps the simplest and most timely contemporary meaning in the Ye Gong story is that we shouldn't let fear of the dragon overwhelm curiosity about China. After all, you don't have to fixate on the People's Republic of China or the Communist Party in order to be curious about Chinese people or their culture. As Jessica Rawson has pointed out, writing not of the nineteenth century and the halcyon days of Mary Gaunt's curios, but of 2023: 'China plays a leading political and economic role on the world stage but, beyond its borders, the country and its history are not well known'. It may be that the more we fear this dragon the less we will ever know. I don't mean there is nothing to fear, far from it; I mean there is everything to learn. We would do well to start over, especially in our education system, arming ourselves against the inevitable accusations of colonialism, orientalism, 'appropriation' and stereotyping with a little of Mary Gaunt's naive curiosity.

When I started writing this, the image of Mary Gaunt and her grandmother's curios was uppermost in my mind. I wanted to defend people who toy with a culture; hobbyists, dilettantes, people who will perhaps never know the 'real thing', the Ye Gongs, who dip into things at a superficial level, shying away from the hard work of getting to know 'reality' through language or history. I meant to say at the outset that these people shouldn't be despised. If interest in something stays at the level of curiosity – fascination – so be it. No harm in that, and in fact when people become too proud of their own level of skill, or too superior in their attitudes to untutored interest, they may be stifling enquiry. I was guilty of that myself during the years when being a 'China expert' meant you were a China gatekeeper, fully authorised to protect your self-ascribed status from intruders. In other words, I went from the innocent fascination of my Rupert books, which I shared freely, to possessiveness, one of the delusions smouldering away with the 'three great fires' of Buddhism; alas, not one of those aroused by my fox-nymph, as she nudged me to the brink of the Dragon Well. An example:

Many years ago I attended a talk by Jung Chang, who was then fascinating Western readers with *Wild Swans*. The hall was packed out, she held the audience in the palm of her hand – and that's not all. She held aloft a pair of 'three-inch-lotus-slippers', once worn on the bound and crippled feet of women like her grandmother. This elicited gasps throughout the venue, necks craning 'like bamboo shoots after the spring rain', straining to get a good look, reminding me of another great moment in the ethnography of costume; my ten-year-old self in 1956, standing not outside the South Australian Museum gazing at bones, but as a furtive would-be spectator inside a fusty, smoke-filled tent at the Royal Adelaide Show, struggling to get a peep at the incrementally revealed flesh of Fatima in her celebrated Dance of the Seven Veils, her modesty, for me at least, guaranteed by the Akubra headwear of much older spectators.

I felt uncomfortable about the Wild Swan slippers, maybe a little holier-than-thou; commercial exploitation of stereotypes etc. I wondered, although there was not so much talk of 'cultural appropriation' back then, if she would get away with these booties if she were not herself Chinese. I now think the problem was not the slippers. They worked well, the audience members were agog, they were ready to learn, but after years of teaching, talking to so many people who had only ever read this one book about China, I came to understand what had really been bothering me. The slippers had bound their minds. They had stayed agog, had not ventured further into Mary Gaunt's 'things beyond', and certainly hadn't made comparisons with fashions and fetishes in human societies of all kinds and ages. They had not pursued the question 'Who but the Chinese?', to which there are some surprising answers. A collector of footwear, on the other hand, even the humblest hobbyist, has the potential to go from unarticulated fascination to rare insights into history.

I don't have a pair of embroidered slippers to accompany my talks, to go with my opium pipes and cricket palaces, but if I did, I would follow their display with that portrait of Ci Xi, and a question – if Chinese men had this bizarre foot fetish, how did the concubine Yehonala, with those intimidating horse-shoes of hers, manage to dazzle the Emperor of China? Then I would show the two glossy Red Detachment women in their high heels and invite the audience to interpret the meaning of these very un-Chinese shoes. Maybe that's why Jung Chang sells millions of books and I am a superannuated academic.

But at the moment I am asking myself another question. I think I may after all, be Ye Gong. In some of my curios I have come face to face with a reality that scares me. Whether I like it or not I will have to let my treasured dreams and memories go before too much longer. How can I deal with that? I can't find an answer in Blofeld, and Werner tells me there *is* no answer. Kidd and Varè tell me to just go on dreaming, while Bob Winter demonstrates the danger of embarking on some quest that may in the end be meaningless, like living to be a hundred.

As I write this and look to my shelves for comfort, I see a photo of me dressed in imperial Chinese regalia, sitting on a dragon throne, a blue dragon and clouds embroidered on the front of my silk costume, and a yellow lantern with the ancient character for dragon beside me. The photo was taken in Kaifeng, China, some years ago. Kaifeng, formerly Bian Jing, was a capital during the Northern Song Dynasty (960-1126 CE). They say it was once, during the eleventh and twelfth centuries, the largest city in the world, famous among other things for its cosmopolitanism, still evident in a few remaining mosques and synagogues. It would appear too, that some of the astronomical devices of the Beijing Ancient Observatory originally came from here, before the fall of the Northern Song dynasty to Jurchen ancestors of the Manchu in the twelfth century.

The city is best known today, however, for an early twelfth century painting, 'Sweeping Tombs Festival on the River', a rare piece of Chinese artistic realism showing all kinds of daily activities taking place in a moment on that ancestor-honouring festival day in Kaifeng almost a thousand years ago (see facing page). You can make out all kinds of stories taking place on a section of the bridge connecting the north and south banks of the river. On the left a man is peering out from a window under which sits a monk with a long white beard, a shoe repairer sits in front of him, the shop

behind is selling ginseng, then there's a writing-brush shop and a fortune-teller's. Over on the right there's a man with a parasol riding a donkey and holding a child; if you look back to the foreground you can see that a girl has fallen over on top of one of the baskets carried on a shoulder pole by a peddler…a moment on the bridge connecting past and present, another world, a thousand years away, and yet all perfectly, humanly, familiar.

I have a copy of the scroll, but it's confined to a beautiful embroidered box, because it's too large to roll out, and anyway, you need to see it in sections; it animates itself as the events of that moment emerge from their silk cocoon. I sometimes unroll it part-way to look closely at scenes like the one above. It was given to me by a dear friend and former colleague, the lady I call 'Little Leaf', although her Chinese given name suggests a whole autumn shower of leaves. It was originally given to her by a fellow Chinese traveller in the United States. My friend didn't know this lady, but it seems she'd lost her purse and had no cash or credit card. Little Leaf gave her some money so she could continue her journey and looked after her until she was able to arrange some funds. Weeks later, back home in Changsha, Little Leaf received a parcel. Her bus companion had sent her a very valuable antique reproduction of the scroll, something that had been in the family for generations. She in turn gave it to me at her PhD graduation ceremony, for which she was resplendent in a Western-style medieval costume and a funny floppy hat. I mention all this because it gives me a clue to the fate of my cabinet of curiosities. For all foreigners in China, for all transients in this world, there are only moments on the bridge. Those moments must be passed on with love and purpose, like Little Leaf's scroll. That may be the only way to honour – or appease – the dragon.

Finally, of the various possibilities, what 'moral' lingers from the tale of Lord Ye and the Dragon? I'm loath to ascribe morals to dragons, and anyway the story, like Chinese poetry, and Chinese paintings, has many blank spaces for the imagination. I would rather search for the *meaning*, not just of the story, but of the dragon itself, as in that quotation at the beginning from *The Book of Imaginary Beings*, the meaning that awaits unrolling, section by section; something of Mongol shamans, Jesuit armillary spheres,

Persian calendars, British opium clippers, The Garden of Perfect Clarity, the Forbidden City, the 'Old Buddha' and her fingernails, incense-burners, fox-nymphs, elephant stables, the Sleeping Dragon Pine in the Ordination Terrace Temple – and The Gates of Dreams.

In the monuments of the ancients, in temples and in the layout of whole cities, even in their ruins, you can discern visions of 'The Heavens', the abode of the gods, intended to invite their presence in the mortal world. In a small way, it's the same with setting up your own cabinet of curiosities. If you want to entice a dragon, real or otherwise, you must first make of your mind a suitable abode for wonder and curiosity – and be prepared to fear what may come to live in it.

Notes

(Illustrations are identified in the text, and when additional information is necessary, in the notes.)

Forethoughts:

Jose Luis Borges with Margarita Guerrero, Foreword to the 1954 Edition, reprinted in *The Book of Imaginary Beings*, Penguin, 2006.

Franz Kafka, *The Great Wall of China*, in *Franz Kafka. The Complete Short Stories*, Nahum N. Glatzer, ed., Vintage Classics, 2018, p. 265.

Freya Stark, Foreword, *Perseus in the Wind*, London, John Murray, 1947.

Bob Winter, Letters, 8 November, 1970.

1: The Sea-chest

'When I was a little girl…', Mary Gaunt, *A Woman in China*, T. Werner Laurie, 1914, p.1.

Ai Weiwei, the contemporary Chinese artist…, Ai Weiwei with Elettra Stamboulis, *Zodiac. A Graphic Memoir*, illustrated by Gianluca Costantini, Ten Speed Graphic, 2024, p.65.

By way of example… see notes on *Wunderkammer*, Ashmole and Tradescant collections, *Wikipedia*.

'The fairy tale tells us…', Walter Benjamin, *Illuminations*, trans. Harry Zohn, Harcourt Brace and World, 1968, p.102.

Marie-Louise von Franz, *The Interpretation of Fairy Tales*, Boston: Shambhala Publications, 1996, pp. 26-27.

Illustration: Photo from Justin Corfield, *The Australian Illustrated Encyclopaedia of the Boxer Uprising 1899-1901*, Slouch Hat Publications, 2001.

'To acquire a first-class knowledge…', Alastair Morrison, *The Bird Fancier: A Journey to Peking*, Pandanus Books, Australian National University, 2001, p.135.

'Though a scattered and disparate lot…', William Lindesay, *The Great Wall in 50 Objects*, Penguin, 2015, p. 6.

'The book may be considered as a series of tableaux…', Blunt, Wilfrid, Foreword, *The Golden Road to Samarkand*, Hamish Hamilton, 1971.

2: Who but the Chinese?

Illustration: Neville John Irons, *Fans of Imperial China*, Kaisereich Kunst, 1982, p. 230.

'But strangest of all…', Arthur De C. Sowerby, 'Cricket Gourds and Culture in China', *The China Journal*, Vol. XVIII, March 1933, p. 158.

We are indebted to Mr Laufer…Berthold Laufer, 'Insect Musicians and Cricket Champions of China' in Fieldiana Popular Series Anthropology, Field Museum of Natural History, Leaflet 37-38, 1948-59, https://www.biodiversitylibrary.org Anthropology Number 22, pp.4-6.

3: Father Hyacinth's Map

'Another perquisite of the keepers was the disposing of the elephants' dung to the ladies of Peking...', L.C. Arlington and W. Lewisohn, *In Search of Old Peking*, p.166.

'From where he stood...', Trevor Hay, *Redgrave's Ghost*, Australian Scholarly Publishing, 2019, p.95.

4: The Scholar and the Beauty

Illustrations: Author collection.

'...delighted more people...', Cyril Birch, *Preface*, Wang Shifu, *The Moon and the Zither: The Story of the Western Wing*, ed. and trans. Stephen H. West and Wilt L. Idema, University of California Press, 1991, p. xii.

'When our heroine appears...' Ibid. xi.

'Turning south'..., Arlington and Lewisohn, pp. 162-163.

5: The Fox-nymph

'It is the animal with the big tail...', *An Animal Imagined by Kafka*, in Jose Luis Borges. and Margarita Guerrero, *The Book of Imaginary Beings*, trans. Andrew Hurley, illustrated Peter Sis, Penguin Classics, 2005.

'After that...', John Blofeld, *City of Lingering Splendour*, Shambhala, 1989, pp. 84-85.

'...shame of self-deception', Ibid., p.90.

6: The Fox Tower

Illustration: From William Cooper Collection: University of Bristol Historical Photographs of China, 2016, University of Bristol Library, Special Collections, reference number: WCO1-182 (152).

'The history of the universe…', E.T. C. Werner, *Autumn Leaves*, Kelly and Walsh, 1928, pp.30-31.

7. The Man of Smoke and Clouds

…'happy hunting ground…', Juliet Bredon, *Peking*, Kelly and Walsh, 1922, p. 410.

…'a Mongolian princess…', David Kidd, *Peking Story. The Last Days of Old Peking*, Clarkson N. Potter, 1988, p.86.

…'a tall amusing man', Ibid.

'Shura had been born a girl…', John Blofeld, *City of Lingering Splendour*, 99-100.

'Letters of Love', review of Diane Armstrong, *The Wild Date Palm* Harper Collins, 2024, in Sunday Life, *Sunday Age*, May 5, 2024.

Paul French, 'Robert Winter, aka Bill Luton', in *China Rhyming. A gallimaufry of random China history and research interests*, chinarhyming.com

Posted April 28th, 2022.

8. The Winter Letters

'…chained to his bed…', David Kidd, *Peking Story*, p. 200.

'…it's painful for me…', Bert Stern, 'One of Us', the Journal of Wabash College, 2024 (on-line college magazine).

'…One of the first things…' Ibid.

Winter certainly sacrificed his own safety…Bert Stern, *Winter in China: An American Life*, Xlibris, 2014 p.336.

'I hesitate…' Ibid., pp. 342-343.

9. 'Who Were You?' An Alternative Obituary

The dates recorded in an obituary, (see https://fr-ca.findagrave. com), containing the ID number of the grave in Ba Bao Shan (Eight Treasure Mountain) cemetery, Beijing, and therefore apparently official, are '31 December 1897 – January [no date] 1987, (aged 99)'. If he was born in 1887, as in the obituary, he would have been 82 in December 1969, not 84 as in the letter of 18 December. Kidd has him 96 in 1981, therefore born in 1885 and, if Winter himself is correct in his letter, he must indeed have been born in 1885. Stern, however, has him 97 in 1984, consistent with an 1887 date of birth. But the letters consistently say something else. In a letter of November 3, 1972 Winter says he will be 86 in December 1972, suggesting a date of birth of 1886, He also says, in the letter of February 5, 1979 that he is 92 plus, making his date of birth December 1886, and this is confirmed in the letter of 15 November 1979, in which he says he is 93 (presumably in the following month). If either the 1885 or 1886 dates are correct, he was in fact either 100 or 101 at his death in January 1987 and his centenary birthday party in December 1987 was well overdue.

'I told them to keep my name out of the papers…',

'I hesitate…',

Bert Stern, *Winter in China*, pp. 342-343.

'Bob Winter had always longed…' Ibid., p.344.

'My time in Peking was growing short…', David Kidd, *Peking Story*, pp. 200-202.

10. Strange Tales from a Foreign Studio

Tale One: Fox-fairies at the Bottom of the Garden

From a tram stop in the West City…', John Blofeld, *City of Lingering Splendour*, pp. 74-82

Tale Two: Skeleton Dancers and Oracles

Illustration: Photograph by Joseph Rock, from Jim Goodman, *Joseph Rock and his Shangri-La, Photographs by Joseph F. Rock,* Caravan Press, 2006, p. 138.

'Dressed in colorful swirling skirts', Ibid., 106-107.

'Some of the Lamas in attendance…', Joseph F. Rock, *China on the Wild Side. Explorations in the China-Tibet Borderlands, Vol 1. Yunnan and Sichuan,* Caravan Press, 2007, pp. 198-204.

Tale Three: Gates of Dreams

'I ordered coffee and eggs…' Daniele Varè, *The Maker of Heavenly Trousers,* Black Swan, 1987, pp. 165-167.

11: Décadence Mandchoue: The Hermit of Peking and the Old Buddha

'The Backhouse Collection in its entirety…', Anne Birrell, *Journal of the Royal Asiatic Society,* Vol 4, Issue 3, November 1994, pp. 451-453, referring to David Halliwell's 'A Catalogue of the Old Chinese

Books in the Bodleian Library. V.1. The Backhouse Collection, 1983.

'...circumstantial yet sufficient proof...', Hugh Trevor-Roper, *Hermit of Peking*, Macmillan, 1979, p.334

'...bronzes, jades, porcelains...' Ibid., p. 305.

'...first button of imperial rank...', Ibid., p. 307.

'...seen even against the lurid background...' J.O.P. Bland and E. Backhouse, *China Under the Empress Dowager*, William Heinemann, 1912, pp. 251-2.

'...if I see a man walking...', William Lewisohn, 'Ching Shan's Diary Remains a Literary Fiction', *Monumenta Serica*, 1940, Vol. 5, No 1/2, pp. 419-427. (Taylor and Francis).

URL: https//www.jstor.org/stable/40725217

'I, Sir Edmund Trelawny Backhouse...', Foreword, D. Sandhaus, (ed.), *Décadence Mandchoue. The China Memoirs of Sir Edmund Backhouse*, Earnshaw Books, 2011.

'I am sure it is quite mistaken...', Alastair Morrison, 'Defending Dr Hoeppli', *The New York Review*, September 15, 1977, in response to an article in NYR by John K. Fairbank, 'The Confidence Man', April 14, 1977.

Reinhard Hoeppli, 'Postscript', in Sandhaus, *Décadence*, p.286

'...not merely erroneous here and there...' Hugh Trevor-Roper, *Hermit of Peking*, p.296.

Illustration: 1903 photo of Ci Xi from Frontispiece, J.O.P. Bland and E. Backhouse, *China under the Empress Dowager*, William Heinemann, 1912.

'Summer Palace Nocturne: the Pastimes of Messalina', is a chapter in Derek Sandhaus, *Décadence Mandchoue*. The reference to 'overflowing carnality' etc. is on p. 59.

Illustration: A 1905 Hubert Vos (1855-1935), portrait of Ci Xi when she was seventy. Vos was a Dutch painter and member of the Royal Society of British Artists.

12. Celestial Theatre

Illustration: Photo from J. Needham, *Science and Civilisation in China*, Cambridge University Press, 1959, vol. III, Plate LXVII, (following p. 450).

Illustration: Photo: Ibid., Plate LII, (following p.370).

'Apart from the Babylonian records...', Ibid., p. 171.

Illustration: Ibid., Fig. 99, facing p. 264, showing 'Purple Palace' to left, and 'Great Bear' to right; constellations in Sagittarius and Capricornus. The stars were drawn in three colours, white, black and yellow.

'One of the most wonderful of these...' Ibid., p. 424.

'Astronomy was a science of cardinal importance...,' Ibid., p. 171.

'Furthermore, as Needham points out...', Ibid., 437.

13. Shadows and Perspectives

Illustration: From 'The Nestorian Stele', *Wikipedia*.

'The controversy is ultimately understandable...', Joseph Lo Bianco, 'Intercultural Encounters and Deep Cultural Beliefs', Chapter 1, in *China and English. Globalisation and the Dilemmas of Identity*, Joseph

Lo Bianco, Jane Orton and Gao Yihong (eds.), Multilingual Matters, 2009. p. 36.

'But what he calls…', Needham, *Science and Civilisation*, vol. 3, p. 448.

'The missions of the Roman Catholic Church…', (and following quotations), W.Y. Fullerton and C.E. Wilson, *New China, A Story of Modern Travel*, Morgan and Scott Ltd., 1909, pp. 243-246.

Illustration: From the cover of *Reminiscences of a Sister, S. Florence Edwards*, E.G. Kemp, The Carey Press, London 1919.

Illustration: Giuseppe Castiglione, 'Qianlong Emperor in ceremonial armour on horseback', coloured inks on silk, c. 1739, from postcard for exhibition, *A Golden Age of China. Qianlong Emperor, 1737-1795*, March-April 2015, National Gallery of Victoria, Melbourne, Australia.

14. The Garden of Perfect Clarity

Illustrations: my souvenirs from the Yuan Ming Yuan; set of stamps and pack of playing cards.

'…survey the world in microcosm.', Geremie R. Barmé, 'The Garden of Perfect Brightness, a Life in Ruins', *Papers on Far Eastern History*, number 11, June 1996, Institute of Advanced Studies, Australian National University, Papers on Far Eastern History, p. 117.

'You can scarcely imagine…', A. Egmont Hake, *The Story of Chinese Gordon*, London: Remington and Co., 1884, p.33. (Hake's father was a cousin of Gordon.)

'I never saw a more pitiable sight…', Ibid., 252.

'Looking up from the entrance of the park...', Ibid., 286-287

'Now back again to Pekin...', Ibid., p. 289.

'One evening five carts...', Hope Danby, *The Garden of Perfect Brightness*, Williams and Norgate, 1950, pp. 198-99.

'It was a clear autumn day...', Ibid., pp 200-201.

See Marcia Reed and Paola Demattè, eds., *China on Paper: European and Chinese Works from the Late Sixteenth to the Early Nineteenth Century*, Getty Research Institute, Los Angeles, 2007, p.108.

15. A Window in the Forest

It was used for tomb ornaments...see Joseph Needham, *Science and Civilisation in China*, Vol IV: 1, pp101-103.

The illustration is from the cover of A. Henry Savage-Landor, *China and the Allies*, (2 vols.), Charles Scribner's Sons, 1901.

The illustration is from A. Henry Savage-Landor, *China and the Allies*, vol. 1, Charles Scribner's Sons, 1901, facing p. 12.

'A party of about thirty Boxers...', 'Fred Whiting in China: Some Personal Observations', From Frederic A. Sharf and Peter Harrington, *The Boxer Rebellion: China, 1900. The Artists' Perspective*, Greenhill Books, London, 2000, .p. 30.

'Whatever the jealousies...', Sharf and Harrington, Ibid., p. 51. The illustration is from a gouache on board drawing by Gordon Browne (from a sketch by a correspondent) published 8 December 1900 in *The Graphic*. Gordon Frederick Browne (1858-1932), was an illustrator of books and magazines. He exhibited landscapes at the Royal Academy London, 1886 and produced a number of Boer War drawings.

It is interesting to note the more recent 'ruins' of a different kind of faith in the vicinity of Guiyang, the 'satellite cities' and theme parks that have sprung up only to be left abandoned, like the 'Evergrande Cultural Tourism City.'

16. Picnic at the Sleeping Dragon Pine: Idylls of Old Peking

'Foreign residents enjoyed Peking all the more…', J.K. Fairbank, 'The Confidence Man', *New York Review of Books*, April 14, 1977 (reviewing Trevor-Roper, *The Hermit of Peking*).

There's another famous book of the time…, see Julia Boyd, *A Dance with the Dragon. The Vanished World of Peking's Foreign Colony*, I.B. Tauris, 2012, p. 183. Boyd notes that Acton made no mention in his writing of the murder of Pamela Werner, despite the fact that he was living in Beijing at the time.

'Chie T'ai Ssu, the Monastery of the Platform of Vows…'. Anne Bridge, *Peking Picnic*, Virago Modern Classics, 1989, p.111.

'The unique thing about these incense burners…', David Kidd, *Peking Story*, p.39.

'They were magical objects…', Ibid., pp. 41-45.

17. The Bamboo Poem

This scroll came into my possession as a gift and I can only assume the rubbing was taken many years ago from a stone in the Forest of Steles, Xi'an., since I have seen it described in a list of the museum's holdings.

18. Curios, Fetishes and the Madness of Crowds

Illustration: Author photograph, Beijing, 2017.

Illustration: Author photograph, Beijing, 2017. I have lost the notes for this photo, but this piece looks to me like the work of Guo Jian (郭建), a Chinese-Australian artist associated with the Cynical Realism Movement that began in Beijing in the 1990s. He has exhibited in China, Australia and internationally and there is a private collection of his work held by La Trobe University, Melbourne (Geoff Raby Collection). I have reviewed some of his work for *RealTime* theatre arts and performance magazine.

'I loved it. We all did…', see Trevor Hay, 'Sex, Drugs and Revolutionary Modern Ballet: Guo Jian, "Mama's Tripping", *RealTime* 42, April-May 2001, p.9. https://www.realtime.org.au/sex-drugs-and-revolutionary-modern-ballet/

'In reading the history of nations…', Charles Mackay, Preface, *Extraordinary Popular Delusions and the Madness of Crowds, Digireads* reprint, 2018 (first published 1841).

Illustration: from *Designs on Chinese Opera Costumes*, Lu Hua and Ma Chiang, Research Studio of North-east Drama Institute, People's Art Publishing House, 1957.

19. Post-Script: A Moment on the Bridge

'Lying awake by her side…', John Blofeld, *City of Lingering Splendour*, p. 90.

'China plays a leading political and economic role …', Jessica Rawson, *Life and Afterlife in Ancient China*, Allen Lane, 2023, xix.

A Curious Bibliography

(Dates in brackets are the original publication dates)

A

Acton, H. *Peonies and Ponies*, Oxford University Press, 1983.

Ai Weiwei with Elettra Zamboulis. *Zodiac. A Graphic Memoir*,
illustrated by Gianluca Costantini, Ten Speed Graphic, 2024.

Airlie, S. *Thistle and Bamboo, The Life and Times of
Sir James Lockhart Stewart*, Oxford University Press, 1989.

Arlington, L.C. and W. Lewisohn, *In Search of Old Peking*,
Oxford University Press, 1987 (1935).

Armstrong, D. *The Wild Date Palm*, Harper Collins, 2024.

B

Backhouse, E. and J.O.P. Bland, *Annals and Memoirs of the Court of Peking*,
William Heinemann, 1914.

Barmé, G. R. *The Garden of Perfect Brightness. A Life in Ruins*,
East Asian History, Number 11, June 1996, Institute of
Advanced Studies, Australian National University.

Barr, P. *To China with Love. The Lives and Times of Protestant Missionaries
in China, 1860-1900*, Secker and Warburg (no date).

_ *A Curious Life for a Lady. The Story of Isabella Bird*, Macmillan, 1970.

Becker, J. *City of Heavenly Tranquillity. Beijing in the History of China*,
Allen Lane, 2008.

Benjamin, W. *Illuminations*, trans. Harry Zohn, Harcourt Brace and
World, 1968.

Birrell, A. *Journal of the Royal Asiatic Society*, Vol 4, Issue 3,
November 1994, pp. 451-453, referring to Halliwell, David,
'A Catalogue of the Old Chinese Books in the Bodleian Library.
V.1. The Backhouse Collection', 1983.
Bland, J.O.P. and E. Backhouse, *China Under the Empress Dowager*,
William Heinemann, 1912.
Blofeld, J. *City of Lingering Splendour: A Frank Account of Old Peking's
Exotic Pleasures*, Shambala (reprint), 1989 (1961).
_ *My Journey in Mystic China. Old Pu's Travel Diary*, trans. from the
Chinese by Daniel Reid, Inner Traditions, 2008.
_ *The Wheel of Life. The Autobiography of a Western Buddhist*, Rider
and Company, 1959.
Blunt, W. *Foreword, The Golden Road to Samarkand*, Hamish
Hamilton, 1971.
Borges, J.L. with M. Guerrero, *The Book of Imaginary Beings*, trans. Andrew Hurley,
illustrated Peter Sis, Penguin Classics, 2006.
Boyd, J. *A Dance with the Dragon. The Vanished World of Peking's
Foreign Colony*, I. B. Taurus, 2012.
Bredon, J. *Peking*, Kelly and Walsh, 1922.
Bridge, A. *Peking Picnic*, Virago, 1989 (1932).
Broomhall, A.J. *Strong Man's Prey*, China Inland Mission, 1953.
Burgess, A. *The Small Woman*, Evans Bros., 1957.

C

Campbell, J. *The Hero with a Thousand Faces*, Princeton
University Press, 1968.
Carl, C.A. *With the Empress Dowager*, KPI Ltd. 1986 (1906).
Chang, J. *Empress Dowager Cixi. The Concubine who Launched
Modern China*, Jonathan cape, 2013.
Clune, F. *Chinese Morrison*, The Bread and Cheese Club,
Melbourne, 1941.
Corfield, J. *The Australian Illustrated Encyclopaedia of the Boxer
Uprising 1899-1901*, Slouch Hat Publications, 2001.
Crow, *Handbook for China*, Oxford University Press, 1984 (1933).
Cui, Guo. 'The Development of Chinese Glass Buildings',
Challenging Glass 2 - Conference on Architectural and
Structural Applications of Glass, Bos, Louter, eds., TU Delft, May 2010.

D

Danby, H. *The Garden of Perfect Brightness*, Williams and Norgate, 1950.
Dorn, F. *A Map and History of Peiping*, Priyang Press,
Tientsin-Peiping, 1936.

F

Fairbank, J.K. 'The Confidence Man', (Review of Trevor-Roper,
Hermit of Peking, in *New York Review of Books)*, April 14, 1977.
French, P. *Midnight in Peking*, Penguin, 2012.
French, P. 'Robert Winter, aka Bill Luton', in *China Rhyming.
A gallimaufry of random China history and research
interests* chinarhyming.com (Posted April 28th, 2022).
Fullerton, W.Y. and C.E. Wilson. *New China. A Story of Modern
Travel*, Morgan and Scott, 1909.

G

Gallenkamp, C. *Dragon Hunter. Roy Chapman Andrews and
the Central Asiatic Expeditions*, Viking, 2001.
Gaunt, M. *A Woman in China*, T. Werner Laurie, 1914.
Goodman, J. *Joseph Rock and his Shangri-La, Photographs
by Joseph F Rock*, Caravan Press, 2006.

H

Hacker, A. *China Illustrated. Western Views of the Middle Kingdom*,
Tuttle, 2004.
Hake, A.E. *The Story of Chinese Gordon*, Remington and Co. Ltd. 1884.
Hay, T. *Tartar City Woman*, Melbourne University Press, 1990.
_ *China's Proletarian Myth. The Revolutionary Narrative and Model
Theatre of the Cultural Revolution*, Lambert Publishing, 2008.
_ *Redgrave's Ghost*, Australian Scholarly Publishing, 2019.
_ *The Library of Lost Horizons. An Antiquarian Voyage*, Arden,
Australian Scholarly Publishing, 2023.
_ *Xun Huisheng*, entry in Leiter, S. (ed.) *Encyclopedia of Asian
Theatre*, Greenwood Press, 2007. Vol. 2, pp. 854-855. See also:
Yangbanxi, pp. 862-863.
_ 'Yellow Lady Meets Black Stump: An Obscene Post-modern
Heroine in Australia', *RealTime* 10, December-January, 1995-96,

pp. 12-13.

_ 'Sex, Drugs and Revolutionary Modern Ballet: Guo Jian,
"Mama's Tripping", *RealTime* 42, April-May 2001, p.9.
https://www.realtime.org.au/sex-drugs-and-revolutionary-modern-ballet/

Holt, E. *The Opium Wars in China*, Putnam, 1964.

Hooker, M. *Behind the Scenes in Peking*, Oxford University Press
1987 (1910).

I

Irons, N. J. *Fans of Imperial China*, Kaisereich Kunst, 1982.

J

Jackson, B. *Splendid Slippers. A Thousand Years of an Erotic Tradition*,
Ten Speed Press, 2000.

Johnston, R.F. *Twilight in the Forbidden City*, Oxford University Press,
1987 (1934).

_ *The Chinese Drama*, Kelly and Walsh, 1921.

K

Kemp. E.G. *Reminiscences of a Sister, S. Florence Edwards*,
The Carey Press, 1919.

Kidd, D. *Peking Story. The Last Days of Old Peking*, Clarkson N. Potter, 1988.

King, M. *China's American Daughter. Ida Pruitt, (1888-1985)*,
The Chinese University of Hong Kong, 2006.

Kuhn, I. *Nests Above the Abyss*, China Inland Mission, 1947.

L

Laufer, B. 'Insect Musicians and Cricket Champions of China'
in *Fieldiana Popular Series Anthropology*, Field Museum of
Natural History, Leaflet 37-38, 1948-59.
https://www.biodiversitylibrary.org *Anthropology* Number 22.

Lee, P. *Opium Culture. The Art and Ritual of the Chinese Tradition*,
Park Street Press, 2006.

Leiter, S. (ed.) *Encyclopedia of Asian Theatre*, 2 vols. Greenwood Press, 2007.

Lindesay, W. *The Great Wall in 50 Objects*, Penguin, 2015.

Listri, M. *Cabinet of Curiosities*, Taschen, 2020.

Lo Bianco, J. 'Intercultural Encounters and Deep Cultural Beliefs',

in *China and English. Globalisation and the Dilemma of Identity*, in
Lo Bianco, J., J. Orton, and Gao Yihong. Multilingual Matters, 2009.
Lovell, J. *The Opium War. Drugs, Dreams and the Making of China*,
Picador, 2011.
Lubbock, B. *The China Clippers*, Brown, Son and Ferguson, 1929.

M

MacGregor, N. *A History of the World in 100 Objects*, Penguin, 2012.
Mackay, C. *Extraordinary Popular Delusions and the*
Madness of Crowds, Digireads, 2018.
McCann, D. 'China's Dream, America's Nightmare', *Quadrant*, May 2024.
McCausland, S. *The Art of the Chinese Picture Scroll*, Reaktion Books, 2023.
McGhee, R.J.L. *How We Got to Pekin, A Narrative of the Campaign*
in China in 1860, Richard Bentley, 1862.
Morrison, A. *The Bird Fancier: A Journey to Peking*,
Pandanus Books, Australian National University, 2001.
_ 'Defending Dr. Hoeppli', (reply to J. K. Fairbank,
'The Confidence Man', April 14, 1977, *New York Review of Books*),
New York Review of Books, September 15, 1977.

N

Naqin, S. *Peking. Temples and City Life 1400-1900*, University of
California Press, 2000.
National Palace Museum. *A City of Cathay*, [Kaifeng], Taipei, 1980.
Needham, J. *Science and Civilisation in China*, vol. III,
Cambridge University Press, 1959.
_ Ibid., Volume IV: 1.
Ng, Chun Bong, Cheung, Pak Tong, Wong Ying and Yvonne Lo.
Chinese Woman and Modernity: Calendar Posters of the 1910s-1930s,
Joint Publishing Hong Kong, 1996.
Nicholls, B. *Bluejackets and Boxers. Australia's Naval Expedition to the*
Boxer Uprising, Allen and Unwin, 1986.

O

Osgood, E. *Breaking Down Chinese Walls*, Fleming H. Revell
Company, 1908.

P

Pearl, C. *Morrison of Peking*, Penguin, 1970.

Peyrefitte, A. *The Collision of Two Civilisations. The British Expedition to China, 1792-4*, Harvill, 1993.

Pruitt, I. *A Daughter of Han; The Autobiography of a Chinese Working Woman*, Stanford University Press, 1967.

_ *Old Madam Yin: A Memoir of Peking Life*, Stanford University Press, 1986.

_ *A China Childhood*, Chinese Materials Center, 1978.

Pu Songling. *Strange Tales from a Chinese Studio*, (聊斋志异), translated and edited, John Minford, Penguin Classics, 2006.

R

Rawson, J. *Life and Afterlife in Ancient China*, Allen Lane, 2023.

Reed, M. and P. Demattè. *China on Paper. European and Chinese Works from the Late Sixteenth to the Early Nineteenth Century*, Getty Research Institute, 2007.

Richie, D, ed. *Lafcadio Hearn's Japan*, Charles E. Tuttle, 2022.

Rock, J. *China on the Wild Side. Explorations in the China-Tibet Borderlands* Volume 1, Yunnan and Sichuan, Caravan Press, 2007.

S

Sandhaus, D. (ed.) *Decadence Mandchoue. The China Memoirs of Sir Edmund Backhouse*. Earnshaw Books, 2011.

Savage-Landor, A.H. *China and the Allies*, (2vols.) Charles Scribner's Sons, 1901.

_ *In the Forbidden Land*, William Heinemann, 1904.

Sharf, F. A. and P. Harrington. *The Boxer Rebellion. The Artists' Perspective*, Greenhill Books, 2000.

Shuck, H. *Scenes in China or Sketches of the Country, Religion, and Customs of the Chinese*, American Baptist Publication Society, 1853.

Sowerby, A. De C. 'Cricket Gourds and Culture in China', *The China Journal*, Vol. XVIII, March 1933

Spence, Jonathan D. *God's Chinese Son. The Taiping Heavenly Kingdom of Hong Xiuquan*, W. Norton and Company, 1996.

Stark, F. *Perseus in the Wind*, John Murray, 1955.

Stern, B. *Winter in China. An American Life*, Xlibris, 2014.

_ 'One of Us', the Journal of Wabash College, 2024 (on-line college magazine).

T

Taylor, P.D. and A. O'Dea. *A History of Life in 100 Fossils*,
University of New South Wales, *2014*.
Thomas, J. *Curiosity. A Love Story*. Emblem, 2010.
Thompson, P. and R. Macklin. *The Life and Adventures of
Morrison of China*, Allen and Unwin, 2004.
Trevor-Roper, H. *The Hermit of Peking. The Hidden Life of
Sir Edmund Backhouse*, Macmillan, 1979.
Varè, D. *The Maker of Heavenly Trousers*, Black Swan, 1987 (1935)
Von Franz, M. L. *The Interpretation of Fairy Tales*,
Boston: Shambhala Publications, 1996.
Voon, C. 'In Ancient China, Pet Crickets Spent the Winter
in Opulent Gourds', *Atlas Obscura*, June 5, 2019.

W

Waley, A. *The Opium War Through Chinese Eyes*,
Stanford University Press, 1958.
Wang, Shifu. *The Moon and the Zither: The Story of the Western Wing*,
ed. and trans. Stephen H. West and Wilt L. Idema,
University of California Press, 1991.
Warner, L. *The Long Old Road in China*, Arrowsmith, 1927.
Werner, E.T.C. *Autumn Leaves, An Autobiography*,
Kelly and Walsh, 1928, pp.30-31.

Z

Zeitlin, J.T. *Historian of the Strange. Pu Songling and the Chinese
Classical Tale*, Stanford University Press, 1993.
Zheng, Yangwen. *The Social Life of Opium in China*,
Cambridge University Press, 2005.

About the Author

D r Trevor Hay is a scholar of comparative and intercultural literature, specialising in Chinese theatre, literature and folklore and in English language writing on China. He is a collector of antiquarian books about China, Central Asia and Tibet and has travelled and worked intermittently in China over fifty years, including a period of UNICEF literacy consultancy with ethnic minority groups, and most recently with a Chinese-Australian group researching Buddhist art in the Dunhuang caves of the Gobi. He has been an Australian Research Council researcher on the teaching of Chinese language and culture for international students and has worked with Chinese community arts and culture groups in Australia, including as narrative consultant for a historical drama society and as an expert committee member for an association for the preservation of intangible cultural heritage. He is a fluent speaker of Modern Standard Mandarin. This is his eleventh book.